What it Feels Like to Die

DEAN BRAXTON

Psalm 23:4 (NKJV)
Yea, though I walk through the valley of the shadow of death, I will fear no evil; For You are with me; Your rod and Your staff, they comfort me.

1 Thessalonians 4:13-14 (NKJV)
But I do not want you to be ignorant, brethren, concerning those who have fallen asleep, lest you sorrow as others who have no hope. For if we believe that Jesus died and rose again, even so God will bring with Him those who sleep in Jesus.

What it Feels Like to Die

Moments in Heaven
Series Book 3

DEAN BRAXTON

What it Feels Like to Die

Moments In Heaven
Series Book 3

Copyright © 2019 by Dean A. Braxton

What it Feels Like to Die

by Dean A. Braxton

Printed in the United States of America

www.DeanBraxton.com

DEDICATION

MAY THE WORK HE'S DONE SPEAK FOR HIM

Dedicated to Lewis Samuel George Braxton, Jr. who was a great dad to me on this Earth. He was born on December 26, 1931, the day after Christmas. He went home to be with God Almighty on April 15, 2017, the day before Easter. He is missed by his family but is celebrating forever with his Lord and Savior, Jesus.

His Wife: Freddie Mae Braxton
His Three Sons: Lewis Samuel George Braxton III,
Gerald Wayne Braxton, and Anthony James Braxton
And the Rest of His Family: 14 Grandchildren, 21 Great-grandchildren,
and 6 Great-great-grandchildren

FORWARD

As Senior Pastor of a church body, I met Dean Braxton through ministry. I heard his miraculous testimony of dying for one hour and forty-five minutes, and I read and recommend this book, *What it Feels Like to Die.*

Dean has an awe-inspiring experience of how he went to Heaven. Jesus looked at him, saw Himself on the inside of Dean, and he was in! We can't save ourselves. Our Heavenly Father sent His son, Jesus Christ, who died for our sins. He was buried and rose from the grave so that sinners through accepting the gospel of Jesus Christ could be reconciled back to the Father for all eternity!

In Dean's book, he explains in great detail how we Christians will journey to our heavenly, eternal home that is prepared only for those who take Jesus as Lord and Savior. Visiting dying Christians and their families is one of the things that I do as a pastor. While talking with dying people, I have noticed that they seem to be focused on the ones they are leaving behind. I have noticed that they are often more concerned about their family members than themselves. Many times, I have also witnessed dying people who are concerned about their loved one's Salvation, especially their children's. After reading Dean's book, I now understand why they weren't focused on death concerning themselves. They had the comfort of Jesus Christ, and He had prepared them for that moment.

Some families, who have lost someone unexpectedly, have expressed to me through their grieving that they wonder if their loved ones are in Heaven.

We all have situations that we have to deal with, whether it is death, grieving, or a broken heart. Some people are living their daily lives without understanding God's plan. Some are suffering pain, sickness, or even relationship problems. Some desire to know more concerning our heavenly, eternal home. Dean's book is for everyone. It is full of hope, peace, and joy; and it answers questions for those desiring to understand what dying and Heaven are like. When finishing this book, I experienced a perfecting in knowing Jesus Christ more fully. This book is a great tool for everyone desiring to encourage others in their questions regarding our journey home.

I, myself, have less fear of dying now. I realize that when it is time to enter my eternal home prepared for me by Jesus Christ, my Lord and Savior, I will not be alone or afraid. This book encouraged me to look forward to the prize of fully knowing and experiencing Jesus Christ. The author causes the reader, through his love for Jesus, to have an opportunity for great satisfaction regarding the going home experience to Jesus Christ and the Father!

Senior Pastor Teri Maher
True Church, Hannibal, Missouri

INTRODUCTION

How many friends do I have who routinely begin a sentence, "In Heaven,…"? One – Dean Braxton. My wife and I met Dean and Marilyn in 2015, and we feel blessed to call them friends. I usually try to ask intelligent questions of people who have had great experiences in ministry so I can glean all I can from them. What do you do when a person has also had the experience of ministry, a great life, death, and being raised and made whole again? You treasure their experience and listen to what they say!

We met at a ministers' gathering where we all discussed many topics. Most of Dean's comments began with "In Heaven,…" For example, "In Heaven, the Father and Jesus are strategizing about how to get everyone on Earth saved." Whenever Dean would speak, I would just want to stop and think about everything that he had said for a while.

I would stop and think about how his experience of dying and going to Heaven rang true with the Scriptures. I knew some of the Bible, but there is something special about hearing about Heaven from someone has been there and come back. His unique insights are biblical but come from the perspective of a human who died and lived to tell about it.

Many of us have wondered what it feels like to die, but there are very few people who can speak from experience. We know that there are many people in the Bible who were raised from the dead, but to actually hold a book written by one who has experienced this is a radical thought! If you are like me, you are curious about what it feels like to die… curious but willing to wait. I think you will be grateful to hear from a believer in Jesus who has been there and done that.

Dean offers insight into the Scriptures that speak into what happens at the death of a believer. His revelation into the Bible on this subject is unique to one who has encountered death and was raised to life.

This book is dedicated to Dean's earthly father – a hint of how important family is to Dean. Dean tells of the importance of family in his experiences in Heaven and explains his drive to see all his family believe so they can be together in Heaven. This book may be about what it feels like to die, but it also helps you FEEL FAMILY!

This book is an encouragement to any believer who fears death! This book is a comfort for those who have "lost" loved ones. This book will tell you what it feels like to die. This book will provoke every believer to tell others about the One who has defeated death.

Pastor Lee Prock
Awakening Community Church, Fredericksburg, Virginia

TABLE OF CONTENTS

Chapter 1

Chapter 2

Chapter 3

Chapter 4

Chapter 5

Chapter 6

I DIED

Clinically Dead, Brain Dead, Biologically Dead

What was it like to die? Have you ever wondered what it would be like to die? Well, I had wondered many times but never thought I would die and then come back and tell people what It feels like to die. You see, I DIED on May 5, 2006. I was what you would call clinically dead. That means that my heart and lungs were not operating. How long was I dead? According to the medical records, I was dead for 1 hour and 45 minutes. I also met the criteria to be called brain-dead because I had no oxygen and blood to my brain for the same amount of time. Medical professionals say that you only need to be without oxygen and blood for six minutes before the brain begins to die. The doctor who was in the room when I died said, "It is a miracle that he is talking and has no brain damage, because he was really, really dead for a long time."

I also fit the criteria for another category of death. That is the category of being biologically dead. After reading my medical records, Dr. Reggie Anderson, the author of *Appointments in Heaven*, told me that after having no oxygen and blood flowing through my body for that length of time, I would have moved into the stage of being biologically dead. He said, "It takes about 17 minutes from when the heart stops to meet that requirement."

According to medical research, signs of being biologically dead are:
1. Respiratory arrest, no breathing – I had that.
2. Cardiac arrest, no pulse – I had that.
3. Brain death, no neuronal activity – I had that.
4. Pallor mortis, paleness which happens15-120 minutes after death – I had that.

One of the signs that I had become Pallor mortis was that my toes looked like dried-up, black scabs of meat. I had no feeling in them. Later, I found out that the doctors were waiting for me to become stronger health-wise so that they could bring me back into the hospital to cut off all ten of my toes.

Prayer Works

The first night I was home from the hospital, my wife, Marilyn, and I decided to work on my toes to see if I could start to feel anything in them. I had gone about a week and a half without having any feeling in my toes after I had been taken off of life support. So, that night, May 16th, after coming home from the hospital, Marilyn decided to soak my feet in a bowl of hot water. As I placed my feet in the water, we both started to pray. My wife was rubbing my feet and toes and praying, when we both saw the old, black-scab skin around the toes start coming off. As the skin came off, I thought to myself, "I have brand-new toes." I remember that later I could not touch my new toes on the floor because of how sensitive they were after that dead skin had come off them. It was like I was walking on a lot of little needles.

You'll Find Out!

To be perfectly clear with everyone reading this book, at the time of my death, I was a Christian. I was and am a born-again believer. I had confessed with my mouth and believed in my heart that Jesus Christ was my Lord and Savior. With all that said, what I'm about to tell you is what it's like to die as a Christian. What you are about to read is the benefit that I received as a Christian. Since I died believing in Jesus Christ, I can tell you with certainty that if you don't know Jesus as your Lord and Savior, you won't get these benefits when you die. You may say, "That is what you believe." All I can say to you is, **"You'll Find Out,** someday." All I am about to share with you is the truth about the way I passed away. I know and you will know sooner or later that what you read in this book is for those who are born again.

Now, before you put this book down, I would encourage you to keep on reading. It won't take you very long to go though it, and what do you have to lose? I've had so many people investigate whether or not I really died. I've had a number of people go through the medical records line by line and come to the same conclusion, I was really dead. I have been on television and radio programs (both religious and nonreligious) telling my story of dying. Many of them had investigated the information from the medical records and talked with medical personnel who were there when I died. They even contacted the actual doctor who was in the ICU room, Dr. Manuel Iregui.

"He Was Really, Really Dead."

Dr. Iregui stated in a TV interview that "It is a miracle – that he's (Dean's) alive, that he is talking with no brain damage. But this is very exceptional, because he was really, really dead for a long time." Dr. Iregui has a great reputation as a doctor in the State of Washington. He specializes in Pulmonary Disease, Internal Medicine, Critical Care Medicine, and Sleep Medicine. He received the Patients' Choice Award in 2011, 2012 and 2014; and he also received Compassionate Doctor Recognition in 2011, 2012, and 2014. I also read that he was one of the top ten doctors in Washington in 2012. As you can see, this doctor should know if person is really dead. [If you would like to view Dr. Iregui's statement about the event, go to DeanBraxton.com or YouTube and watch the television show that was put together by Christian Broadcasting Network (CBN) 700 Club.]

Another unique experience that I had was when a national television program wanted to do a story on Near Death Experiences (NDE). They were out to prove that anyone who said they had a NDE was lying. They chose me to be one of the people who they were going to expose as not telling the truth about what had really happened to him. They wanted to show that I didn't really have an encounter with the afterlife. But, after researching my story, they informed me that I had been disqualified to be a part of the TV program because my story was "too true." So, once again, it was proven that I had died on May 5, 2006.

As you have read in the previous paragraphs and will read in Chapter 6: "Medical Records and Medical Transcripts," it can be proven that I died.

In my travels throughout the United States and around the world, almost every time that I speak, I inform people that I can prove that I died. The doctor who was in the room when my death took place said: "He was really, really dead for a long time." I have had so many people investigate the incident who have come to the same conclusion – **I DIED!** The medical records and medical transcripts have recorded it as Prolonged Cardiac Arrest for 1 hour and 45 minutes.

Should You Start Reading Chapter 2?

People can say that I didn't go to Heaven, but I went somewhere. So, I would encourage you to keep on reading this book to find out what it is like to die. I encourage those of you who are not Christians to skip the rest of this chapter and start reading at Chapter 2: "My Story of Dying." What do you have to lose? It is a short read that could possibly impact the rest of your life on this earth. Remember that everyone is going to die sooner or later. Here is your chance to read a story about a person who did die.

Again, if you are not a Christian, please start at Chapter 2. If you want to read the rest of this chapter too, you are more than welcome to.

Who Should Read On?

The rest of this chapter is for those who say that they are Christians but who don't believe that I could have died, gone to Heaven, and come back to this planet. We all know that every one of us is going to die sooner or later. I really like the way the Bible says this in the following verses.

We Will All Die Someday

Psalm 49:10 (NET)
Surely one sees that even wise people die; fools and spiritually insensitive people all pass away and leave their wealth to others.

Job 34:19-20 (NET)
...who shows no partiality to princes, and does not take note of the rich more than the poor, because all of them are the work of his hands? In a moment they die, in the middle of the night, people are shaken and they pass away. The mighty are removed effortlessly.

So, we will all die someday.

Dying and Going to Heaven

Now, if you don't believe a person can die, go to Heaven, and come back; please read on. I believe that I can clear this up for you. Let's make sure you understand that if you read this and still do not believe that this happened to me, that is okay. I don't save anyone or get them into Heaven, only Jesus does. As long as you are born again, you still get to go to Heaven. If I beat you into Heaven and you see me there, you are not going to come up to me and say, "You were right!" You are going to say, "You were way short in describing this place (Heaven)!" The only thing that I can tell you right now is that the account you are about to read is from a man who was born again, a man who was and is a true believer in Jesus Christ as Lord and Savior, a man who had the Holy Spirit residing on the inside of him when he died to this earth. I just want to tell you what it was like to die as a Christian. I can't tell you what it would be like to die as a person who doesn't know Jesus Christ as Lord and Savior; I can only tell you what it was like to die as a person who does.

Is It Appointed Once to Die?

One of the biggest questions that people have about my dying experience is about the verse that comes out of Hebrews 9:27.

Hebrews 9:27 (NKJV)
And as it is appointed for men to die once, but after this the judgment,

Book of Hebrews

The book of Hebrews was written to inform the Jewish converts of the true gospel, to show that Jesus came to complete the law. It tells us that what Jesus did was not to modify the Law of Moses but to overrule and dissolve it.

So, for us to really understand Hebrews 9:27, we must read Hebrews, Chapters 1-12. This will give us a better picture of Hebrews 9:27.

Let's look at Hebrews 10:16-18.

Hebrews 10:16-18 (NKJV)
"This is the covenant that I will make with them after those days, says the Lord: I will put My laws into their hearts, and in their minds I will write them," then He adds, "Their sins and their lawless deeds I will remember no more." Now where there is remission of these, there is no longer an offering for sin.

Who Was Judged For Us? Jesus

To sum it all up, Jesus paid the price for our sins and has forgotten them. Because of his forgiveness and forgetting, we have been judged through Jesus Christ. There is no judgment for us who are born again, we who are saved from damnation. I challenge you to read the book of Hebrews and see what God has done for you.

We also find this same thing in Colossians 2:13-14.

Colossians 2:13-14 (NKJV)
"And you, being dead in your trespasses and the uncircumcision of your flesh, He has made alive together with Him, having forgiven you all trespasses, having wiped out the handwriting of requirements that was against us, which was contrary to us. And He has taken it out of the way, having nailed it to the cross."

There was a time when we all deserved God's judgment, for we were guilty of breaking His law. But, as you read, Christ took ALL our sins upon Himself; and He endured the judgment that we deserved, which was death.

2 Corinthians 5:21 (NKJV)
For He made Him who knew no sin to be sin for us, that we might become the righteousness of God in Him.

So, "It is appointed for men to die once but after this the judgment." Jesus Christ took our judgment on the cross. For some of us who are Christians, the fact that Jesus took our judgment is hard for us to handle. This is what the writer of Hebrews was trying to get across to the Jewish people who were used to having to work to be saved. For many of us, it is the same way... work, work, and work some more to be saved.

Not of Works

Ephesians 2:8-10 (NKJV)
For by grace you have been saved through faith, and that not of yourselves; it is the gift of God, not of works, lest anyone should boast. For we are His workmanship, created in Christ Jesus for good works, which God prepared beforehand that we should walk in them.

So, some people might ask, "If it is not by works, then why should we do the things of God?" The reason is: "If you are a Christian, act like one." This is what I always say in response to this question.

We must understand that everything that God created acts in the nature that it was created in. Trees act like trees; flowers act like flowers; cows act like cows; dogs act like dogs; cats act like cats; and so on, and so on. Everything created by God acts in its nature. We who are born again, we who confess Jesus as Lord and Savior, we who have the Holy Spirit living in us, we who are in Christ, we are all new creations. "Old things have passed away; behold, all things have become new." **Act Like Who We Are!**

2 Corinthians 5:17 (NKJV)
Therefore, if anyone is in Christ, he is a new creation; old things have passed away; behold, all things have become new.

If it is true that we are new creations in Christ, then we need to act like it. God has given us His Spirit to live within us to help us in that nature.

John 14:26 (NKJV)
"But the Helper, the Holy Spirit, whom the Father will send in My name, He will teach you all things, and bring to your remembrance all things that I said to you."

Appointed for Men to Die Once

Now that we have covered the "judgment" of Hebrews 9:27, let's look at the "dying" part of this verse.

One thing that I want to make mention of about dying in verse 27 is that it is talking about Jesus dying once for us all.

We can also read about this in Hebrews 2:9.

Hebrews 2:9 (NKJV)
But we see Jesus, who was made a little lower than the angels, for the suffering of death crowned with glory and honor, that He, by the grace of God, might taste death for everyone.

Here it says that Jesus died for everyone, including you and me. He not only died your spiritual death; He also died your physical death. Here we see judgment and death are all in one package. So, that "appointed once to die and then the judgment" has been taken care of if you are born again.

Others Who Died and Came Back

For if it is appointed unto man once to die, then what about the following 10 incidents of people dying in the Bible and coming back to life? I ask you to take the time to read some of these accounts.

OLD TESTAMENT: 1 Kings 17:17-24 (Widow of Zarephath's Son), 2 Kings 4:18-37 (Shunammite Woman's Son), and 2 Kings 13:20-21 (Israelite Man)

NEW TESTAMENT: Luke 7:11-17 (Widow of Nain's Son); Luke 8:49-56 (Jairus' Daughter); John 11:1-44 (Lazarus); Matthew 28:1-20, Mark 16:1-20, Luke 24:1-49, John 20:1-21 (Jesus Christ); Matthew 27:50-54 (Saints in Jerusalem); Acts 9:36-42 (Tabitha or Dorcas); and Acts 20:7-12 (Eutychus).

All of these accounts are about people who died and then later came back to life on this planet.

Life Extended

In the Bible, we can also read about King Hezekiah, whose life on Earth was extended by God.

Isaiah 38:1-5 (NKJV)

In those days Hezekiah was sick and near death. And Isaiah the prophet, the son of Amoz, went to him and said to him, "Thus says the Lord: 'Set your house in order, for you shall die and not live.'" Then Hezekiah turned his face toward the wall, and prayed to the Lord, and said, "Remember now, O Lord, I pray, how I have walked before You in truth and with a loyal heart, and have done what is good in Your sight." And Hezekiah wept bitterly. And the word of the Lord came to Isaiah, saying, "Go and tell Hezekiah, Thus says the Lord, the God of David your father: 'I have heard your prayer, I have seen your tears; surely I will add to your days fifteen years.'"

Lives Shortened

There are also those whose lives have been shortened on Earth, as mentioned in both Proverbs 10:27 and 1 Corinthians 11:28-30.

Proverbs 10:27 (NET)

Fearing the LORD prolongs life, but the life span of the wicked will be shortened.

1 Corinthians 11:28-30 (NET)

A person should examine himself first, and in this way let him eat the bread and drink of the cup. For the one who eats and drinks without careful regard for the body eats and drinks judgment against himself. That is why many of you are weak and sick, and quite a few are dead.

What Did We Learn?

Here we have it. Other people have also died and come back to life on Earth. One man's life was extended for 15 years, and some people's lives have been shortened for one reason or another. These examples make "appointed for men to die once" take on a whole new meaning.

What About Me?

I went home before my time. It was because of a doctor's mistake, not Dr. Iregui's. I had a kidney stone stuck on my right side, and it caused a kidney infection. The doctor gave me antibiotics, which he thought would take care of the infection, but they did not. The doctors didn't check to make sure that the infection was gone before they did the operation. So, when they broke the stone to pieces, it released the infection/poison into my blood stream; and I became septic. Everything in my body started to die. According to the medical records, 29 different organs were impacted and started to die or shut down. The first to go was my lungs, which caused my heart to stop. The medical records state that my heart stopped for 1 hour and 45 minutes, which qualified me as being clinically dead.

As I stated before, I can prove that I died. That's the easy part, 1 hour and 45 minutes, that's what the medical records say. Dr. Iregui who was in the room said, "He was really, really dead." But because I was born again, because I knew Jesus Christ as Lord and Savior, and because I had the Holy Spirit residing on the inside of me, I did what Christians are supposed to do when they leave their body or die. I went to be with God the Father and Jesus. See, I had confessed with my mouth and believed in my heart that Jesus Christ is Lord. I just want you to know that it's not unusual that I would go to Heaven. That's what happens to Christians when they leave their bodies.

This happens because Jesus said we will go to the place where He is.

John 14:1-6 (NKJV)
"Let not your heart be troubled; you believe in God, believe also in Me. In My Father's house are many mansions; if it were not so, I would have told you. I go to prepare a place for you. And if I go and prepare a place for you, I will come again and receive you to Myself; that where I am, there you may be also. And where I go you know, and the way you know." Thomas said to Him, "Lord, we do not know where You are going, and how can we know the way?" Jesus said to him, "I am the way, the truth, and the life. No one comes to the Father except through Me."

Prayer for Salvation

I know that I have done things that were wrong, and I am sorry for all of them. I believe Jesus died on the cross for all my wrongdoings. I ask you, God, to please forgive me for all of them right now. I now receive you as my own Savior and Lord. With your help, Father God, I will try to please you every day of my life from this day forward. In Jesus' name, I thank you for saving me.

Chapter 2

My Story of Dying

In the Hospital

I can remember moving through a hallway very fast. I was thinking to myself, "Where are we going?" The thought came to me that something must be wrong. As I tried to take in more oxygen, the smell and taste of the plastic mask that was covering my mouth and nose came along with inhaling of the air into my body. Even though the air was going into my lungs, it felt like it was not helping. I started to wonder what was happening to me as I looked at the hospital walls that were passing by. And every wall I went by seemed to have many doors, windows, and open corridors. There I was, struggling to breathe, and yet, I was evaluating all of my surroundings. An IV pole was being pushed or pulled alongside my bed as I was being wheeled down the hallway. There were people pushing the bed from behind and a person who seemed to be pulling it at the same time. Then there were the people on both sides of the bed directing what needed to be done. I saw all of this as I needed more air in my body.

Once again, I was saying to myself, "Something is wrong here and I am in the center of this situation." While still smelling that plastic mask, I notice that no one around me was smiling. All the medical staff had serious looks on their faces. I knew that they knew what was going on, but I couldn't ask because of the mask that was over my mouth. As one light faded away, the next light overhead came into my focus. How fast I was moving, I didn't know, but it was fast.

I did know that I was still having breathing problems. They started when I was in the recovery room. I remember waking up after the operation and having a hard time taking air in. At that moment, I had just had one of those nasal tubes put into the nostrils of my nose. I complained to my wife and the nurses who were taking care of me. I heard one of them ask me, "Mr. Braxton, Mr. Braxton what is wrong?" I seemed to go in and out of sleep, but I finally got across that I needed more air. That is when they gave me the plastic mask to go over my mouth and nose. Someone said, "Let's see if this will work." As they checked on me, I remember saying, "I am not getting enough air."

As I was being wheeled through the hospital, I was surrounded by medical people who were looking very serious. I still couldn't breathe that well. It even seemed to have gotten worse. I was having a hard time breathing at that moment. Every breath that I was taking in didn't seem to be adequate enough to fill my lungs. It reminded me of the time that I had almost drowned, and then I said to myself, "I am dying!"

I Almost Drowned

Then my lungs were having a hard time taking in oxygen. The memory of almost drowning was coming back to me. At age six or seven, I was with my older brother at his friend's house. We were swimming in a big pool at the time that was ten feet deep. I remember watching my brother, who was three years older than me, dive into the deep end. His friend was older than him by a year, and he was diving in too. I watched them, time after time, dive off the diving board into the deep end of the pool. I was thinking to myself that I wanted to try it. They looked like they were having so much fun. Every time I got close to that end of the pool, my big brother would stop me. I felt like he was just bossing me around. He liked to do that back then. So, when he and his friend were occupied with something else and not watching me, I snuck over to the diving board and jumped in.

I remember the sound of the splash and how I could not touch the bottom to stand up so that my head would not go underwater. In the other end of the pool, I could stand up. If I wanted to put my head underwater, I could; but I had the power to bring it up for air. Here, there was no bottom to stand on, and I did not know how to swim. I recall that I started to flap my arms and sink. It was not long before I was underwater looking up seeing the blue sky through the water. I could not breathe at all, I remember tasting the water in my mouth as I sank in the pool. I was going down fast, and I started to laugh. This was my reaction whenever I was frightened as a kid. Then as I was sinking, I saw my brother breaking the plain of the water. He grabbed me, and he and his friend pulled me out of the pool. I don't know if they were saying anything to me, but I knew I was gasping for air. I don't think they said anything to my brother's friend's mother at the time. I believe that was because, if she had found out about what happened, we would not have been able to go and swim there anymore. I do remember having a hamburger after this incident that day.

What I Would Tell God

Because of this event of almost drowning, I never wanted to go through something like that again. I had a great fear of suffocation. All I had up to that time of coming close to dying was the incident of almost drowning, until then. There I was being wheeled though the hallways fast at St. Francis Hospital in Federal Way, Washington, when I thought of that time of almost drowning. Whenever I thought about drowning, I was overtaken with great fear.

I did everything I could to hide my fear from people who were Christians. I remember after becoming a Christian, I really didn't want anyone to know about it, not even my wife. I knew that God knew and that the devil knew. I would talk to God and try to get Him to agree with me that when I died it would not be because of lack of air. I even tried to make a deal with God to get Him to agree with me that when I died, it would not be by suffocation. I tried to let Him know that I could die another way, like being shot in the head, falling off a cliff, being run over by a car, or the best way, in my sleep, and just wake up in Heaven. Just how many times I talked to God about this, I can't remember. All that I can tell you is that I was afraid to die. I just thought it would be awful and really terrible if it was by suffocation.

No Fear

I had the terrible experience of almost drowning and had great fear overall of dying. When I thought to myself, "I am dying," the emotional awakening that I experienced can't be put into words. Because of the lack of air coming into my body, I knew that I was dying. Just why I was dying, I didn't know. Even when I said that I was dying, it was like a statement and a question at the same time. What took place with the words in my thoughts was outside of anything I could have believed.

First, I didn't know that I would not have fear. To me, because I knew that I was dying, I thought that I should have experienced it differently than I did. After I thought the thought that I was dying, great overwhelming joy rose up on the inside of me. I knew that I was dying, but I wasn't having the reaction that I had believed I would. I thought I would have a reaction of being hysterical, being panicky, or even having an overwhelming feeling of being freaked out. But there I was with this great joy, this pure calmness, this happiness. I really was surprised at the next words that I said, "I'm going home." Where did these words come from? Why did I say these words at that moment of knowing I was dying? Previously, I had no idea that I would say those words. I had been certain that I would experience what I wrote about before: fear, panicking, and freaking out, but I didn't. Those words seemed to come from inside my belly, from my most inner part, the essence of who I am. As those words emerged from within me, they came with peace, joy, and love just for me. Did these feelings come before or after the words "I'm going home"? I don't know. I just knew that I was going home, and peace, joy, and love overtook me.

Understanding the Truth

I have always believed that I was a spiritual person on the inside of a body, but I found out that I was a spirit with a body on the outside. When I realized I was going home, I felt that I was separated from my body at that very moment. I was not a body with a spirit but a spirit surrounded by a body. I understood the truth about myself. When I said, "I'm Going Home," those words seemed to unlock an understanding of who I was. I questioned where those words had come from. Yet, they are words that were life to me, eternal life. They were so real that I knew that my spirit only could come to that awareness by the help of the Spirit of God who lives within my spirit, the "real" me.

These eternal words, "I'm Going Home," brought with them a knowledge that I knew that I was going to be with God Almighty. I knew I was going where Jesus is. I knew that I was going to have the Holy Spirit inside my spirit forever. I was going home. I knew, that I knew, that I knew where home was; and it was not Earth. And with that great knowing came an understanding that I didn't want anyone to stop me. There seemed to be a pull – a great pull on me to be with Jesus and

Father God. It was like I was incomplete because I was not with them in Heaven. But I knew I was complete with the Holy Spirit living on the inside of me. I just knew with those words that I was more connected to God than I had realized I was in the past. That connection came when I was born again, but for some reason, I wasn't aware of how strong it really was. I just knew fear was gone, and I wanted to be with my Lord and Savior forever.

As I was still being wheeled down the hallway in the hospital bed, I pondered over how I just wasn't afraid. As I got weaker and weaker, the peace got stronger and stronger. I didn't question it. I didn't wonder about it. I just knew that I was on my way home. Again the joy, unspeakable joy, was increasing through my entire being; and I didn't want anything or anyone to stop it. The pull on me became stronger at every moment. The pull to be with Jesus Christ was growing within me. The pull to be with the Father, my Father, my Heavenly Father grew, along with the smile I had on the inside because of knowing that I was going home.

Another Hospital Room

Finally, we all entered into the room they were taking me to. I saw a new doctor, not the same one who worked on me for the kidney stones. I didn't know why this different doctor was there, but there were also other medical personnel around him, along with my wife. This doctor was facing Marilyn, and he talked to her first. Then he turned and looked down at me, and in a very slow and low voice, he said that he needed my permission to put a PICC line in me. I looked at Marilyn and asked her if this was something that we should do. She said, "yes," so I gave them permission to do the procedure. I didn't even know what a PICC line was, and I remember them trying to tell me about it. But when my wife said that it was okay, I thought that everything was going to be alright. That was the last thing that I remembered when I was on Earth.

The White Window

The next moment, I knew that I was headed to that big, white window (what looked "LIKE" a window) that was ahead of me. I knew that was where my home was. I knew that was where

Jesus was. I knew that I was going to where my Father was, my Father, my Heavenly Father; and I wanted to be with Him. As I was leaving my hospital room, I remember hearing all the commotion that was going on around me, but I was paying no attention to it. I was only focused on that window that was before me – that bright light. I knew that I was moving towards it very fast. Was I flying, or was I just being transported to Heaven? It is hard to put into words exactly what I was really doing. I just know that I was moving very fast because everything around me seemed to fade away as I moved towards that window of light. I didn't care if I was walking, running, hopping, jumping, gliding, or flying. I just knew that I was going home!

I can remember leaving the hospital room, heading up through the ceiling, going through another room and ceiling, through another room and ceiling, and then through another room and ceiling. How many ceilings and rooms did I go through? Maybe five, six, or seven at the most. I really wasn't counting. As I was leaving the hospital, I remember reaching the roof of the building and not looking back at all, just heading toward that window of light.

I knew I was moving through blue sky, but the window of light seemed even brighter than the blue sky. The color of the sky seemed to be a pure blue with dirty spots all throughout it. That window of light was brighter than the sun. I knew I was on my way home, and I was not going to stop for anyone or anything.

I remember that when I entered outer space, I went past the planets. They all seemed so little. I don't know why, but they just seemed to be very small to me – Jupiter, Saturn, and Neptune. I knew that I was headed home and that window was so bright with light. It was not a small window that got larger as I got closer to it. Even when I first saw it, it looked like a big window. It didn't even seem like it was very far away because I was there in no time at all. Time was not a factor in how fast I was moving. I just knew that I was moving fast – very, very, very, very, very, very fast. I knew that I was going home to be with Jesus and the Father. I JUST WANTED TO BE HOME!

Prayer for Salvation

I know that I have done things that were wrong, and I am sorry for all of them. I believe Jesus died on the cross for all my wrongdoings. I ask you, God, to please forgive me for all of them right now. I now receive you as my own Savior and Lord. With your help, Father God, I will try to please you every day of my life from this day forward. In Jesus' name, I thank you for saving me.

Chapter 3

Does the Bible Support My Story of How I Died?

My Thinking

Dying was nothing like I thought it would be. I had all kinds of preconceived ideas of what it would be like and what I would go through. Now that I have experienced death, I realize that I was so wrong in all the aspects of what I thought it would be like. What I had been told and had read was just plain wrong. I thought that born-again believers in Jesus would go through the same thing as nonbelievers in Jesus. Again, I was so wrong. It was different, and I knew that was because of what Jesus had done for me. You can say, "That is just your belief system," but I will say to you, "You will find out." Every person will leave Earth sooner or later (die). I did, and I'm sharing with you what I experienced.

As I said in Chapter 1, I can prove that I died. Medical records say that I was dead for 1 hour and 45 minutes. Dr. Iregui said that I was "really, really dead for a long time." All this is covered in Chapters 1 and 6. What I experienced and where I went is covered in Chapter 2. In Chapter 3, you will read how I processed dying after coming back to this planet, Earth. I didn't want to come back to the planet because this place has so many issues. I was in a place that had no problems; everything was right; it was past peace. There was nothing to be peaceful from, and I fit!

Understand the Way that I Died

First, understand that the way that I died was the one way that I didn't want to die because I had almost drowned as a young child. According to the medical records, I suffocated. My urinary tract was blocked by a large kidney stone, which caused a bacterial build up. If anyone else had the same problem and the bacteria/infection was released into their bloodstream, they would have died, too. That is what happened to me. Later on, I was told by the doctors and medical professionals that I had become septic. My medical records and transcripts revealed the same thing. I had experienced septic shock.

More than 1.5 million people get sepsis each year in the United States. About 250,000 Americans die from it. According to the Centers for Disease Control and Prevention, one in three patients who die in a hospital have sepsis. Septic or septic shock is a serious medical condition that occurs when sepsis, which is organ injury or damage in response to infection, leads to dangerously low blood pressure and abnormalities in cellular metabolism. It can cause multiple organ dysfunction syndrome (formerly known as multiple organ failure) and death. That is what happened to me. It caused multi-organ failure and death. One of the systems that failed was my lungs. They shut down because of the poison/infection. I remember the feeling of knowing I was dying because of not getting enough oxygen in my body.

Soon, my lungs just stopped working, and I suffocated. As I already mentioned in Chapter 2, suffocation was the one way that I absolutely didn't want to die. After becoming a Christian, I remember many times thinking about dying. The number one way that I didn't want to go was suffocation. I absolutely didn't want to ever go through that again – experiencing not being able to breathe. After I became a Christian, I had conversations with God about dying. And I am very sure that suffocating was a non-negotiable experience that I never wanted to go through again. I remember giving God suggestions on how I could die. As I stated earlier, the number one way that I wanted to die was by just falling asleep one night and waking up in Heaven. Another way that would have been okay was to have something quiet and without any pain. I didn't know what that would be, but I was negotiating with God. He would know how I could die without pain. Death because of lack of oxygen was not on my list of possible plans for dying. As I said before, I did not want to die by suffocation. Many times, I thought to the myself that the worst way to die would be suffocation.

Why Me?

There I was in my hospital room thinking to myself about how I had died. I could remember how hard it was to breathe in the recovery room, thinking it was only for a moment, "This will not last that long." I also remember how the nurses were giving me more oxygen and how they moved me from a nasal cannula to an oxygen mask to get more air into my lungs. At the time, I didn't think much of it. To me, everything was okay. So, I had no fear at that moment. Going over that situation in my mind, I had thought, "My breathing isn't as good as it could be, but there is no way that I will die." I had only had a kidney stone procedure. I had a similar procedure for kidney stones four years earlier, and I didn't have any problems at all. I thought to myself, "Why would I have trouble at this point?" These were the thoughts that were running through my mind while I was in the recovery room.

My wife was there by my bedside; she would know if something was going wrong. We both had no worries. I would look at her every once in a while and think, "Everything is okay." I just needed to catch my breath. I was not thinking about dying at all, and I sure didn't think that I would be dying that day, May 5th, 2006, but I did.

One of the first things that I thought about after I was taken off of life support was why I had died. As I was in my hospital room after everything took place three to six days later, I still was asking the question, "Why did I die?" All I could remember was that I had gone into the hospital to have a kidney stone taken care of. There I was at another hospital and had died, and dying was nothing like I thought it would be. Was it because I had gone to Heaven, and Jesus had tried to wipe everything out of my head so I wouldn't have to remember how bad it really was to suffocate? Was it the medications that they gave me that took out my memory so that I could not remember what took place? And yet, I remembered leaving my body; I remembered leaving the hospital; I remembered leaving outer space and going into that dark area which was so thick that I knew that only my spirit could go through it, not my fleshly body. I remember the prayers that were passing me by like I was standing still, and yet, I knew I was moving fast. I knew my body had died, and my spirit (the real me) did not die. How could I remember and know about so much that I had no clue about before?

Being Born Again

Being born again meant so much more than I thought it did before this experience. There was a lot that I had not known or understood previously, and what dying was like was part of it. I no longer had any fear of death. I saw dying as Paul said, "For to me, to live is Christ, and to die is gain" (Philippians 1:21 NKJV). For I had experienced joy, unspeakable joy, and peace that passes all understanding. I had touched eternity and loved it. It was not like I thought it would be. How could that be? I had been born again for a long time. I had accepted Jesus Christ at the age of 17. At that time and now 30 years later (at age 47), there I was understanding what it means to die as a Christian. All those years of having it totally wrong – Why was that? Why did I have it totally wrong? I had read my Bible many times, including the verses about dying. I had an understanding, I thought, of what it would be like to die. But there I was, pondering about my death; and yet, it was nothing like I thought it would be.

No Fear

The first thing that was different than I had thought it would be was that I had no fear, none at all. I had heard that people who die have smiles on their faces or looks of peace. I thought that happened because their spirits had left their bodies, and they were finally not experiencing any pain. In those final hours of fighting with death, they gave up the ghost (spirit), and there was that peace.

There were also accounts of Christians who had been martyred. I remember reading stories and listening to testimonies about people who had been martyred for Jesus Christ. How strong these people were, to die for their faith! I thought that they must have prayed and fasted a lot and read their Bibles every day. I used to think to myself that I'd better read my Bible more; I'd better fast and pray more; I'd better be kind more, because if I was called to die for God, I would have to be stronger. For at the moments when I would think about dying either naturally or as a martyr, I always had fear come on me. I was afraid to die.

Yet there I was, after going through death, knowing that I didn't have any fear at all. How could that happen? I remember being pushed really fast in a hospital bed down a hallway. I remember saying to myself, "I am dying." I remember that all of a sudden I had joy, peace, and comfort come all over me. I remember saying, "I am going home." Did the joy, peace, and comfort come before I said this or after? It seemed like it all came at the same time. Everything happened so fast. The joy, peace, and comfort hit me all at the same time. When I really think about it, they seemed to be there before I said, "I am dying, and I'm going home." I realized that they had been on the inside of me for a long time. Jesus had placed them in me when He came into my life so I didn't need to strive to be ready for that moment.

Joy
John 15:11 (NKJV)
These things I have spoken to you, that My joy may remain in you, and that your joy may be full.

Peace
John 14:27 (NKJV)
Peace I leave with you, My peace I give to you; not as the world gives do I give to you. Let not your heart be troubled, neither let it be afraid.

Comfort
John 14:16 (KJV)
And I will pray the Father, and he shall give you another Comforter, that he may abide with you forever;

Your Spirit Leaves and Your Body Dies

Then I knew these had come because Jesus loves me; and because He loves me, I didn't have to earn them after I accepted Him as my Lord and Savior. Another thing that took place was that I knew that I had left my body and then my body had died. At first, I didn't know how to explain this to others. I had no idea that this was going to take place. I always thought that your body died first and then your spirit left, but it didn't happen that way. Sometimes I tell Christians that if they were to fall off of a tall building, before they hit the ground and died, their spirits, the real them, would leave. Why? Because if you're body is going to die, your spirit will leave your body before you hit the turf or pavement. It took me about two and a half years to find scriptures in the Bible that prove what happened to me.

Beyond and Back

One of the events that led me to find the evidence in the Bible was when someone finally asked me what it was like to die. It happened in 2011, Marilyn and I were being interviewed for a TV show called *Beyond and Back* (put out by the Biography Channel). At that time, the show was very popular. We were in Hollywood, California, taping the episode. The director asked me many questions. One was: "What was it like to die?" They wanted to know what I felt physically and emotionally. I thought about it for a long time because, truthfully, I didn't think that I had died. So, I started talking about how I wasn't there when my body died. I got to tell them that I had joy, peace, and comfort come all over me. I remember that after I told them that, the director and cameraman looked at me like I was crazy. I didn't think they believed me. I do know, when they aired the program, the answer to that question was edited out.

The End of the Spear

What that question did for me was open my mind's eye to recognize anything that would relate to how I had died. All of my senses were enhanced to notice things that could help explain how I had died. If anything I read came close to supporting what I had experienced or proved that what I was saying was true, I wanted to know more about it. I was still using "falling off the building" for some time as the example to explain what happened when I died.

In 2012, I had just come off a 14-day trip to Singapore where I was sharing my story of going to Heaven. I didn't plan well because two days later I was headed on a 6-hour drive to the mountains in western Oregon to do a men's conference. One of the nights at the conference, they showed a movie entitled *The End of The Spear*. This movie was about tribesmen in the Ecuadorean Rainforest who massacred a group of men who were missionaries. Sometime after the killings, they abandoned violence and embraced the families of the men whom they had killed. One of these family members was a young boy whose missionary father had been slain. After his father had died, he and his mother moved to the village to minister to and live among the tribesmen. The story went on to tell about the boy growing up in their village, becoming part of the tribe, and staying as a young adult to minister to them. In the process, he became really good friends with one man in the village, but he didn't know that this was the very man who had killed his dad. Near the end of movie, the tribesman who had speared his dad to death, took the boy, who by this time had become a young man, to the place on a river where he and others had killed the missionaries. The tribesman said, "It happened here. They didn't shoot us. There is more you need to know. I saw them."

The son asked, "Saw what?" The scene then goes back in history and shows the native men trying to destroy a plane with the son's father having a spear sticking out of his belly and bright lights hovering over the airplane.

The tribesman said, "Your father saw them also. Your father was a special man. I saw him jump the Great Boa while he was still alive."

When I read those words on the screen, because they had tribesmen speaking in their own language and captions in English for us to read, I was in awe. When he said, "I saw him," the son's father, "jump the Great Boa while he was still alive," I knew what he was talking about.

See, to "jump the Great Boa," in the tribesman's culture, meant entering the afterlife. He said, "I saw his spirit leave." The son's father's spirit left his body before his body died here on Earth. The tribesmen saw the missionary's spirit going to Heaven even when the man's body was alive on earth. I wanted to jump out of my chair. All I could say to myself was, "I understand, I understand, I UNDERSTAND." That was the first time that I had heard about someone else who had a similar experience of dying like I did.

China's Book of Martyrs

Now, I was on a quest to see if others had that same experience. I remember many people who witnessed someone dying saying that they saw their spirit leave, but up to that time, no one had said the person's body was still alive on the planet for a short time and then had stopped breathing. The next place where I saw stories like mine was in a book entitled *China's Book of Martyrs* by Paul Hathaway. In that book, there were many accounts of things happening that were similar to the story that I heard when watching the movie, *The End of The Spear.* What I wanted was to find something in the Bible that said that this is what happens to Christians when we die. I knew there had to be some Bible verses that support this experience but where?

The Body Without Your Spirit

One day, as I was reading my Bible, a verse jumped out at me and I said, "There it is!" The scripture that said the spirit must leave first for the body to die. I found it in James 2:26.

James 2:26 (NKJV)
For as the body without the spirit is dead, so faith without works is dead also.

So simple... Yet, I had read the faith part of the verse for years and overlooked the spirit part. There are two truths to this verse. One, "faith without works is dead." That is true, but "the body without the spirit is dead" is the other truth. There it was: our spirits have to leave our bodies first before they die. Wow!

There is also Genesis 2:7 where we find out that Adam was not alive until God breathed into him. God had to place a spirit in him for Adam to become a living being. Wow, again!

Genesis 2:7 (NKJV)
And the Lord God formed man of the dust of the ground, and breathed into his nostrils the breath of life; and man became a living being.

The meaning of "breath" is "spirit" in the Hebrew.

So, here it is again in the scriptures that I had previously read over and over. Because of having this experience of dying, I saw these verses differently than I had in the past. I saw where this man, Adam, didn't even become a living soul until after God breathed into him the breath of life. So, this body that I am in right now (everybody's in a body) really can't live without my spirit, but my spirit can live without my body. Most people have never experienced dying, so they don't know that their bodies can't live without their spirits. Even Christians act as though their bodies are more powerful than their spirits that live on the inside of their flesh, but it's the other way around. Their spirits are more powerful than the bodies that they're encased in.

I found this out when I died. My body was dead because the spirit being who I really am had left. Now, my body knows that it cannot live without my spirit, the real me, but I can live without my body. Sometimes when I have a small mystery pain in some part of my body, I say in a joking way to my body, "If you don't act right, I'm leaving."

No Pain in Dying

One day, while reading my Bible, I found out why I had died, yet didn't feel the pain of death. I experienced leaving my body, and it died, but I did not.

Again, it was so simple... found in Hebrews 2:9.

Hebrews 2:9 (NET)
...but we see Jesus, who was made lower than the angels for a little while, now crowned with glory and honor because he suffered death, so that by God's grace he would experience death on behalf of everyone.

Hebrews 2:9 (NKJV)
But we see Jesus, who was made a little lower than the angels, for the suffering of death crowned with glory and honor, that He, by the grace of God, might taste death for everyone.

Death (Greek): that separation (whether natural or violent) of the soul and the body by which the life on earth is ended.

Suffering (Greek): something undergone, i.e. hardship or pain; subjectively, an emotion or influence: affection, affliction, motion, suffering.

Taste (Greek): a primary verb; to taste; by implication, to eat; figuratively, to experience (good or ill): eat, taste.

Here, I saw in this verse where it said that when Jesus died, he died my death. What I saw was not just my spiritual death but also my physical death. This is why I didn't feel any pain. Because Jesus, when He died on the cross, felt the pain for me. He went through the physical suffering that I should've gone through. He suffered my death along with taking all my sin. He paid my price for judgment as I stated in Chapter 1. He did this for me. He went through the suffering and pain of that final death of my body as well. I can remember being in Heaven and saying to Jesus, "You did this for me." One of the things that I was talking about is that He died for me so that I would not have to die spiritually or feel the physical pain of the moment that my body died. Again, all I can say is: "Wow!"

Here is another scripture that says that Jesus Christ paid for us physically so that we would not experience sickness.

1 Peter 2:24 (NKJV)
...who Himself bore our sins in His own body on the tree, that we, having died to sins, might live for righteousness— by whose stripes you were healed.

So, here it is. It's in the Scriptures. I was supposed to be experiencing this. This is the way Christians die, or better yet, leave this planet. We are not supposed to feel the "sting of death." We are not going to physically die like a person who is not born again.

1 Corinthians 15:55-58 (NKJV)
"O Death, where is your sting? O Hades, where is your victory?" The sting of death is sin, and the strength of sin is the law. But thanks be to God, who gives us the victory through our Lord Jesus Christ. Therefore, my beloved brethren, be steadfast, immovable, always abounding in the work of the Lord, knowing that your labor is not in vain in the Lord.

Sting (Greek): a sting, as that of bees, scorpions, locusts.

I didn't feel any pain during those final moments because Jesus Christ took the sting of death from me.

Again, I Had No Fear

Because I didn't experience any fear while dying, I wish that I could give that same peace of mind that I received then, to everyone else. But I did acquire the gift of informing all people on Earth of who can give them the ability to have no fear when they die. This benefit comes only through Jesus. He offered it to all people. As I stated before, when I realized I was dying, there was no fear. I had joy, unspeakable joy, peace that passes all understanding, and great comfort. Again, there was a reason why these attributes of God came all over me when I was dying. They had always been on the inside of me from the time that Jesus placed them there when He came into my life. The other reason that I had no fear was because of what Jesus had done. In Hebrews 2:14-15, the writer said that Jesus died for all of us so we would not fear death.

Hebrews 2:14-15 (NKJV)
Inasmuch then as the children have partaken of flesh and blood, He Himself likewise shared in the same, that through death He might destroy him who had the power of death, that is, the devil, and release those who through fear of death were all their lifetime subject to bondage.

Fear (Greek): fear, dread, terror.

Jesus, through His death, destroyed Satan/Devil who had the power of death so that we, all humankind, would not have the fear of dying. Because I was born again, I could not fear death because of what Jesus had done. As I like to say, "It came with the package." "Not fearing death" will present itself to every Christian in that moment when it is needed. I did not have to work for it. "Not fearing death" came with the grace of God.

Ephesians 2:1-10 (NKJV)
And you He made alive, who were dead in trespasses and sins, in which you once walked according to the course of this world, according to the prince of the power of the air, the spirit who now works in the sons of disobedience, among whom also we all once conducted ourselves in the lusts of our flesh, fulfilling the desires of the flesh and of the mind, and were by nature children of wrath, just as the others. But God, who is rich in mercy, because of His great love with which He loved us, even when we

were dead in trespasses, made us alive together with Christ (by grace you have been saved), and raised us up together, and made us sit together in the heavenly places in Christ Jesus, that in the ages to come He might show the exceeding riches of His grace in His kindness toward us in Christ Jesus. For by grace you have been saved through faith, and that not of yourselves; it is the gift of God, not of works, lest anyone should boast. For we are His workmanship, created in Christ Jesus for good works, which God prepared beforehand that we should walk in them.

Experiencing Death like God Said

Here it is in the Bible – my experience of dying. I went through it just exactly like God said I was supposed to. I wasn't to go through it with any fear of death. Jesus Christ took care of the fear of death on the cross. I was supposed to leave my body and then it would die, but the real me, the spirit that I am inside this body, was not to experience the sting of death. When I accepted Jesus Christ as Lord and Savior, whether I believed that I would die the way the Bible said did not matter. Because I was born again, I still received the benefit of what Jesus did for me. It had nothing to do with my belief system, it had everything to do with what God had promised.

Leaving Earth/Passing Through

The last thing that I experienced was that I left this body and it died. As I went home (to Heaven), I remember leaving the hospital so fast. I left Earth faster than the speed of sound. I passed through the whole universe faster than the speed of light. I went through that space where there is no light (complete darkness), before entering the window of light in a blink of the eye.

How fast I was moving can only be measured as the Bible says in 2 Corinthians 5:6-8.

2 Corinthians 5:6-8 (NKJV)
So we are always confident, knowing that while we are at home in the body we are absent from the Lord. For we walk by faith, not by sight. We are confident, yes, well pleased rather to be absent from the body and to be present with the Lord.

Absent (Greek): to go abroad, emigrate, depart, to be or live abroad.

2 Corinthians 5:6-8 (NET)
Therefore we are always full of courage, and we know that as long as we are alive here on earth we are absent from the Lord – for we live by faith, not by sight. Thus we are full of courage and would prefer to be away from the body and at home with the Lord.

I came to understand the magnitude of just how fast I was moving. There really are no English words to describe the speed. I've come to understand that if I say, "faster than the speed of sound," that is too slow. If I say, "faster than the speed of light," that is still too slow. I have to say it the way the scripture says it, "to be absent from the body is to be present with the Lord and at home."

Being an Ambassador For Christ

I always understood that this place which we call Earth, which I like to call "the planet," is not my home. When I became born again, I was told that this planet was not my home. I felt that way at the beginning of my journey of growing to be more Christlike, but I can't tell you when I first really understood it, when I first heard it preached to me, or when I first read it in the scriptures. I had heard words like "sojourners" and "ambassadors," and phrases like "we are just passing through this old Earth," we who are Christians. But I really can't tell you that I truly understood what I read and heard and what it really meant for me personally.

When I said those words, "I am dying, I'm going home," I knew this old Earth was not my home. I understood that we who are born again are on our way home, and this is the journey that we need to take to get there. It became very clear. I knew I was on a pathway as I ventured home. I knew this was my Heavenly Father's plan for me so that I could be the most effective on this planet for Him. Now, I know that if I stray from the exact path, I will still get to go to Heaven. The path did not save me nor will it save me. Jesus is the only One who can save a person. When I got to Heaven, Jesus looked at me, saw Himself on the inside me, and I was in.

So, this is the pathway my Father God wants me to walk on this planet so that I can reach as many people as possible for Him, to be that "Ambassador for Christ." Now, I understand that this was not and is not my home. Where Jesus and God the Father IS, that is my true home, and the Bible says this over and over again. If you are born again, this is not your home.

John 14:1-6 (NKJV)

"Let not your heart be troubled; you believe in God, believe also in Me. In My Father's house are many mansions; if it were not so, I would have told you. I go to prepare a place for you. And if I go and prepare a place for you, I will come again and receive you to Myself; that where I am, there you may be also. And where I go you know, and the way you know." Thomas said to Him, "Lord, we do not know where You are going, and how can we know the way?" Jesus said to him, "I am the way, the truth, and the life. No one comes to the Father except through Me."

2 Corinthians 5:1-5 (NKJV)

For we know that if our earthly house, this tent, is destroyed, we have a building from God, a house not made with hands, eternal in the heavens. For in this we groan, earnestly desiring to be clothed with our habitation which is from heaven, if indeed, having been clothed, we shall not be found naked. For we who are in this tent groan, being burdened, not because we want to be unclothed, but further clothed, that mortality may be swallowed up by life. Now He who has prepared us for this very thing is God, who also has given us the Spirit as a guarantee.

2 Corinthians 5:17-19 (NKJV)

Therefore, if anyone is in Christ, he is a new creation; old things have passed away; behold, all things have become new. Now all things are of God, who has reconciled us to Himself through Jesus Christ, and has given us the ministry of reconciliation, that is, that God was in Christ reconciling the world to Himself, not imputing their trespasses to them, and has committed to us the word of reconciliation.

Philippians 3:17-21 (NKJV)

Brethren, join in following my example, and note those who so walk, as you have us for a pattern. For many walk, of whom I have told you often, and now tell you even weeping, that they are the enemies of the cross of Christ: whose end is destruction,

whose god is their belly, and whose glory is in their shame—
who set their mind on earthly things. For our citizenship is in
heaven, from which we also eagerly wait for the Savior, the Lord
Jesus Christ, who will transform our lowly body that it may be
conformed to His glorious body, according to the working by
which He is able even to subdue all things to Himself.

2 Timothy 4:17-18 (NKJV)
But the Lord stood with me and strengthened me, so that the
message might be preached fully through me, and that all the
Gentiles might hear. Also I was delivered out of the mouth of the
lion. And the Lord will deliver me from every evil work and
preserve me for His heavenly kingdom. To Him be glory forever
and ever. Amen!

Hebrews 11:13,15-16 (NKJV)
These all died in faith, not having received the promises, but
having seen them afar off were assured of them, embraced them
and confessed that they were strangers and pilgrims on the
earth. And truly if they had called to mind that country from which
they had come out, they would have had opportunity to return.
But now they desire a better, that is, a heavenly country.
Therefore God is not ashamed to be called their God, for He has
prepared a city for them.

1 Peter 1:3-5 (NKJV)
Blessed be the God and Father of our Lord Jesus Christ, who
according to His abundant mercy has begotten us again to a
living hope through the resurrection of Jesus Christ from the
dead, to an inheritance incorruptible and undefiled and that does
not fade away, reserved in heaven for you, who are kept by the
power of God through faith for salvation ready to be revealed in
the last time.

As you have just read in these scriptures, you can see
that Earth is not our real home. We are just passing through.

Window of Light

So, what about the window of light that I passed
through? I have always said that it looked "like a window"
because that is the best way I can describe it. I've heard some
people describe it as "a light at the end of the tunnel." But for me,

it looked like a window, a big lighted window. Was it that? No. In the book of Revelation, John referred to it "a door opening up to him." Then he got to see into Heaven.

Revelation 4:1 (NKJV)
After these things I looked, and behold, a door standing open in heaven. And the first voice which I heard was like a trumpet speaking with me, saying, "Come up here, and I will show you things which must take place after this."

But for me, from the time I left the hospital to the time I entered into Heaven, it looked like a big, bright light at a window. This is the closest way that I can describe it.

When I entered in, everything was right, and I was home. Everything was right; it was past peace; there was nothing to be peaceful from; and I was home.

Prayer for Salvation

I know that I have done things that were wrong, and I am sorry for all of them. I believe Jesus died on the cross for all my wrongdoings. I ask you, God, to please forgive me for all of them right now. I now receive you as my own Savior and Lord. With your help, Father God, I will try to please you every day of my life from this day forward. In Jesus' name, I thank you for saving me.

Chapter 4

Why We Have Hope

In Chapters 4 and 5, I want to cover how I now see death from a heavenly point of view. These chapters go over in detail "Why We Have Hope" and "Why We Grieve." I pray that they will help those of you who have had a loved one leave the planet or die to understand why you do not react like those who are not born again. There is both sadness and joy, at the same time, competing for a position on the inside of us. Most of us who call ourselves Christians do not understand that we can have both emotions and still be happy for our loved one(s) in Heaven.

First, let us look at "Why We Have Hope."

1 Thessalonians 4:13 (NET)
Now we do not want you to be uninformed, brothers and sisters, about those who are asleep, so that you will not grieve like the rest who have no hope.

The Greek verb, κοιμάω (koimaw), literally means "sleep," but it is often used in the Bible as a euphemism for death when speaking of believers.

How Would I Respond to Others Dying?

After I came back to this planet, I did not think any of my friends or family members would die before I went back to Heaven. But since that time, I have watched friend after friend leave Earth. Even as I have been writing this book, I have had four good friends die. Steve Mix, Donald Levesque, George Noland, and Marie Knox (my cousin) all went home to be with their Father God. I have even had other family members who have passed from this planet including uncles; an aunt; and even my dad, Lewis Samuel George Braxton, Jr. So, death has not stopped since I had my experience.

I can remember being in my hospital room in ICU, saying to myself and hoping God was listening, "I do not want to be insensitive when the people who I love die, especially family members." I remember how I had responded when people who I had known had died prior to my having this Heaven experience. I had wondered how I would respond and act if my wife, kids, parents, or brothers died. Back then, I didn't know what I would do. The closest I had come to experiencing how I might feel was when my grandparents, uncles, aunts, and very close friends had died. But I was still lacking the full impact of knowing what it would be like when someone I had known and had contact with every day for years, died.

First Person to Die After My Death

My first response to a friend dying after I came back to Earth was with a man named Ray Osborne. We were good friends when we both lived in the Seattle area. We went to the same church, attended men's events together, and went fishing from time to time. Our families were very close for about seven years. He and his family moved away, and we had little contact with them for the next four years. Then, one day I received a message on Facebook from his daughter that said that he had died. I can remember thinking to myself that no one who I knew was supposed to leave this planet until I returned back to Heaven. I did have sadness for him, but I also knew he went to Heaven. I thought about how happy he was. I wasn't guessing. I knew it! Then I thought about how blessed he was to go before I got to returned "home." I was happy for him – no more pain of living on this Earth. I wasn't thinking about physical pain, although he did have some. For as long as I had known him, he had severe asthma. I was thinking about how much pain this Earth gives out that we have gotten used to. Most people don't even recognize it. We just live in it. I did grieve for him, but it was really not for him but for his wife and kids. I knew that they would miss him very much.

After the death of Ray, I had another incident that opened my eyes to the role I would play on this planet when it came to people dying. Many times, I have been asked to talk with people who have been diagnosed with terminal illnesses and are likely to die within a few weeks or months.

Gloria Strout

It started with a 12-year-old little girl named Gloria Strout. I met her and her parents through a good friend named Tom Curran. He oversees an organization called "I Love My Catholic Faith." He was one of the first people who had me come and share about dying and going to Heaven. Tom invited some Catholic Faith people to come to his house and hear my story. At his gatherings, there would be anywhere from 15–25 people there to hear me speak. This is where I first met the Strout family.

Gloria had been fighting cancer for a few years before I met her. To this day, all that I can remember about her is how beautiful she looked. A few months after we first met, I was asked by Tom if I could go to Seattle Children's Hospital to see her. She was struggling to live and had a question for me about Heaven. I asked Marilyn, my wife, to go with me; and she agreed, so we went.

A few days later, I remember entering that hospital in Seattle with Marilyn and seeing all the children who were there. The first thoughts that went through my mind were, "Why was I totally healed?" and "Why are these children not healed?" Then I was thinking about the diversity of how many different ages, races, and ethnic groups where there. I thought about how Satan does not discriminate in handing out his pain. Why do we, God's children, separate in how we fight Satan and his kingdom. That was the first painful scene I had seen on Earth since I had died. It played over and over again in my head back then. I already didn't like being back on this planet, and that experience didn't help.

As we moved through the hospital to Gloria's room, there were kids everywhere, young ones and older ones, and as I said before, so many different groups. Seeing them brought back a memory of when my son, Gabriel, was sick at age two and a half. He had a disease that elderly people get, and because of that, we were in emergency rooms and hospitals a lot for two months. Doctors were trying to figure out what was wrong with him. I remember one night as he was going potty, some of his intestinal lining came out in the potty bowl. I thought some big worm was living on the inside of my son. Later on, I was told it was intestinal skin lining. During that time, I didn't care about what was going on in life. I just wanted my son healed. After many emergency room visits and overnight stays in the hospital, they found out what was wrong. The doctors gave him some medication and said he would be fine in days, but it actually took about two months for him to get well.

So, to see all kinds of kids and their parents was hard for me as I walked to Gloria's room. All I did as I walked there was pray. We finally got to her room. As I looked in, I saw that there were a number of medical professionals in there. One of them came out and asked us to wait in a room down the hallway and said that when they were done one of them would come to get us. As we went to the other room and entered it, we sat down. As I sat there, I thought about what I would say. How would I bring hope in this situation? As I was thinking, I saw the door open and Gloria's father, Doug, walked in. He greeted us very warmly, with a smile. I thought to myself as we finished greeting each other, "I have to say something." But before any words could come out of my month, Marilyn said, "Tell us about your daughter." Doug's face lit up, and he said that we were the first to ask him that question. He told us about all the hospitals he had been in with his daughter and all doctors who had never asked him that question. He was thankful for all they had done and were doing, but he wished that just one of them would have asked him that question. So, he told us about his little girl for next 45 minutes. During that time, Gloria's mother came into the room, and she looked like a woman who was going through great stress.

Before Doug could finish telling us about his daughter, someone came in and told us she was ready for us. Again, we had seen many different children in that place, but right then I was focused on what I would say to Gloria. As we entered, the room had a number of medical personnel in it but I didn't care who was in there. My focus was on the beautiful little girl before my eyes. She was hooked up to monitors that had the normal beeping sounds you hear in a hospital room. Marilyn and I came to her left side. I told her how beautiful she was, and my wife said something to her. I let her know why I came. She had questions for me, and her parents wanted me to talk to her about Heaven. She smiled. I let her know that I also had to pray for healing. She smiled again, showing her teeth this time, but she was very weak. I asked her what questions she had for me.

She asked, "Can I see my family from there?" I said that if God wants you to, you can. She smiled and relaxed. That was the only question she had. Then, Marilyn and I prayed for healing for her.

We left the hospital, and within two weeks, she went home to be with Jesus. Later, I was told by her dad and Tom, that from that time on, whenever they visited her, she had peace until she passed. Doug said that this was because of my answer to the question she had asked me. Later, her parents started a foundation, Gloria's Angels, which helps lift burdens and build communities so people can focus on caring for loved ones with life -threatening conditions.

I Hate Death

Since that time, I have communicated with so many people about kids, spouses, relatives, friends, and coworkers who have died. I have also talked to many people who were dying, but Gloria's "going home" helped me to identify why I hated death. It was not that she went to Heaven; it was that she and her family would be separated for a while.

It was clear that being separated from each other was not God's plan. We are apart from each person who we love through death because of a man, Adam, eating from the tree of knowledge of good and evil (Genesis 2:15-17). This was not God's original plan for the human race. He had planned in Genesis 1:26-28 for us to be together forever as families.

Lewis Samuel George Braxton, Jr.

It became even more apparent to me how much I hated death when my own dad left Earth on April 15, 2017, the day before Easter of that year. He was 85 and was born December 26, 1931, the day after Christmas. This was the first person in my inner, inner, inner circle to die.

That was the test for me of how I was going to react to having someone so close to me die. I had him in my life for 59 years, and I didn't know what it was like not to have him here. Over the years, with any major decision in my life, I would call him with questions and for advice, and he was always there for me. I can still remember his answers to this day. I have passed them on to my children, grandchildren, and others.

He and my mother gave me a great childhood. I have good memories of growing up in both Winton and Atwater, California. When I was a child, my dad was an officer in the United States Air Force as a navigator on B-52 bombers. He had been on a number of other airplanes in his career, but by the time I came around, it was B-52s. After he retired as a Major, he went to work for Merced County in the probation department. For me, both of those professions were impressive when I became an adult. But as a child growing up, he was just my dad. He did a great job in protecting and guiding us, my three brothers and me, from the afflictions of the time, mainly racism. He placed himself in the community as a person who was an integrated part of the areas where we lived. I only new my dad as a community leader. At one time, when I was growing up, he was the head of both Little League baseball and Cub Scouts. Later in my life, when I was a teenager, he was elected to the Atwater School Board; and when I was in my late twenties and early thirties, he was elected to the Merced Community College Board. He stayed on that board for many years and was the representative for the West Community College board along with the National Community College board at times. The one civic service group that he was involved in, from the time I was five until the time he died, was the Lions Club. He enjoyed that group the most. There are a lot more things that he was involved in that I am still finding out about. He loved to help people through his many activities, but he also helped me as his son. Because of what he did, my brothers and I are still benefiting from his life on Earth.

I knew my dad loved me, and I knew he loved my brothers. So, when he started to leave this planet, I found out how I would take it. I found out that I was not insensitive.

Dad Dying

During the last week of February 2017, I received information that my dad was not doing very well. My older brother, Lewis, called and told me that they had taken dad to a hospital in Turlock, California, which was located about 30 minutes from where he lived. At the hospital, it was determined that he had pneumonia and that he would stay there until it had cleared up. I did not think that much of it at time. To me it was a speed bump in the road. He had health issues for the prior 15-20 years. Every time he had come out of them well. So, I thought that we could pray him out of this one too. I prayed and sent texts out to people asking them to pray for him. I had a number of people who I could count on who would be in agreement with me for him to recover. As I prayed over him, I prayed for the rest of the family for safety and healing, as well.

That week, I was in Nashville, Tennessee, and Bowling Green, Kentucky, doing services. That Saturday, I did a service in Nashville. We saw people come to Jesus, recommit back to Jesus, and be healed. I see this happen at most of the services that I speak at. To me, this is what Jesus does. After I got back to the little house I was staying in next to the church where I had spoken that morning, I had a thought, "What if my dad does not make it this time?" I pushed the thought out of my head and went on with the rest of the day. That night, I went to sleep without thinking about. The next morning, the thought came again. I didn't do anything with it. I put some music on that I had downloaded in my phone and started to get ready to go to Bowling Green, Kentucky, to do a service there. But the thought about my dad got louder. "What if he doesn't recover?" Then the song "Even If" by MercyMe came on. I sat at a table in that little house and listened to that song over, and over, and over again. I must have listened to it for at least an hour or two. I remember wiping tears from eyes. The words matched how I was feeling at the time. Here I was, facing the possibility of someone in my inner circle dying. This would be my first, big loss of someone who I was a part of and who was a part of me. I knew my dad loved me, but I also knew that if he did not want to be here on Earth, I could not stop him from leaving. That is when I knew that I would really have to fight for him to stay. Fight what? Fight death.

He Stopped Eating

During the next week, the reports from my brother were not good. Dad had stopped eating in the hospital and wanted to go home. I had already planned to be in California from March 2-13. I had planned on doing services from March 4-12 in a number of churches. I called the person who had organized the services and let him know that I would only be doing services on the weekends. So, he canceled all my week-night services.

As I kept in touch with my older brother, he let me know that Dad would be going home at the same time I would be arriving. As it happened, he would be home for two hours before I could get there. This was perfect timing for me so that I could help take care of him. I became his caretaker for the next two weeks, except on weekends. I left on Fridays to do services on Saturdays and Sundays for three weekends in a row.

I enjoyed taking care of my dad for that short time. What I didn't like was watching my mother lose her husband who she had been married to for 63 years. That was very hard. But I got to show my dad how much I loved him every day that I was with him.

Family Who Had Died

One time when we were alone, I asked him if he had seen any of his family members who had died since he had gotten sick. The reason I asked him this question was because at one time he had told me about every family member he had been with before they had died – that they had seen family members who had already passed away come to them and tell them about Heaven. Those who had died would start talking to them as if they were in the room with them. He knew that they weren't hallucinating.

He said his own mother had gone through that scenario. He was talking to her, and she started calling out people's names and talking to them. My dad said that he knew the people she was talking to had been dead for a long time, but his mother could see them and talk to them. I believe that this happened to him so that he could witness a heavenly visitation from family when he was with his mother for the last time on Earth. He knew, after that incident with his mom, that she was going to die. Not too long after he got back home, she did die.

This conversation came up after I told him about his sister, Aunt Barbara, the one I thought was in hell. But when I got to Heaven, there she was shiny, smiling, and having pure joy. I apologized to him for making that judgment about his sister. Of course, he forgave me. I told him she must have accepted Jesus into her life because that is the only way you get into Heaven.

So, I wanted to know if he had seen any family members since he was in the hospital or at home. He knew why I asked, and he said, "no," but he was having dreams about the end of time. He started to tell me what he was experiencing, but my mother came in the room, and he shut up. The whole time that I was there, we were never alone again to talk about it. Later, he did tell me that he was tired of the fight. He was ready to go. I knew he meant dying. I knew that he had heard me talk about Heaven and what I had experienced many times.

Tired of Fighting

I remember, after he told me that he was tired of fighting and ready to die, I went outside and cried. I cried because my dad, whom I had with me my entire life on this planet, was now going to be leaving me. He wanted to die. Even though I cried, I still could pray and have others pray, and I did. The last day that I saw my dad alive on Earth was March 10, 2017.

As I think about it now, I still have great memories of taking care of him in those two weeks. After I left, I didn't cry anymore. It was settled in my heart where my dad was going. He had let me know eight years earlier that he was born again. He had accepted Jesus Christ in his life as Savior and Lord.

He Was Not Dead to Me

April 15, 2017, I received a call and was told that my dad had left the planet. I was with Marilyn and my grandchildren, Gabrielle and JJ, coming back from Indiana after visiting with some friends. For some reason, I didn't mourn at that time. I knew my dad wasn't dead. I had felt that feeling before with close friends who had died but didn't think that much about it.

But this time it was with my own dad, and I knew he really wasn't dead.

When I present my story of dying, this is a statement that I often say: "I did not die, my body did." Now at that moment of finding out that my dad had died, I was feeling this very strong on the inside of me. My dad was not dead, just his body was.

When I went to the funeral, I can remember seeing and feeling the loss others were having, but I didn't have the same experience that they were having. My dad was not dead, only his body was, and I knew it. I could see the loss in others who knew my dad. But I didn't have that loss; I had hope.

I Had HOPE

That verse in 1 Thessalonians 4:13 about the hope we have as Christians when a loved one leaves Earth made more sense. See, in the spirit, I am still connected to my dad. In John 15:5, Jesus said, "I am the vine; you are the branches." Because of this connection through Jesus Christ, we who are born again are connected spiritually forever.

John 15:5 (NKJV)
"I am the vine, you are the branches. He who abides in Me, and I in him, bears much fruit; for without Me you can do nothing."

There is a lot more to this in John, Chapter 15. I just want to point out that we who are saved through Jesus are also connected through Him forever. So, even if a loved one who is born again leaves this planet, we are still spiritually connected to them. I cover this more in Chapter 5.

This doesn't mean that they are Jesus and have special powers. We are not to worship the person at all. We are only to worship Jesus and Father God through the Holy Spirit. Remember, you who are born again can go directly to God.

Hebrews 4:14-16 (NKJV)
Seeing then that we have a great High Priest who has passed through the heavens, Jesus the Son of God, let us hold fast our confession. For we do not have a High Priest who cannot

sympathize with our weaknesses, but was in all points tempted as we are, yet without sin. Let us therefore come boldly to the throne of grace, that we may obtain mercy and find grace to help in time of need.

We are never to seek after a loved one when we have Jesus. We who are Christians have the hope that we will see them again, living in and through Jesus.

It is well with our souls!

Prayer for Salvation

I know that I have done things that were wrong, and I am sorry for all of them. I believe Jesus died on the cross for all my wrongdoings. I ask you, God, to please forgive me for all of them right now. I now receive you as my own Savior and Lord. With your help, Father God, I will try to please you every day of my life from this day forward. In Jesus' name, I thank you for saving me.

Chapter 5

Why Do We Grieve?

What I Learned from My Dad's Death

Today is April 15, 2019, two years after Dad left this planet (died). He went to be with his Heavenly Father, the Lord Jesus Christ, with the Holy Spirit residing on the inside of him forever. When my earthly father died, I learned a lot by grieving over him. Since this was the first person who I had experienced dying who I was so close to, I took the time to really move through the grieving process. I also took the time to see how others in my family went through and/or are still going through this process.

I had other people around me who were either close friends or family die, but my dad was the closest ever. When my grandparents went home to be with Jesus, I felt the sorrow of having them gone, but I also had the joy of knowing them on this planet. But dad was in a different category altogether. He was the one person outside of my mother and older brother, who knew me the longest on Earth. So, my connection to him would naturally be different.

I thought, because of that, it would hit me harder when someone of my inner circle (wife, children, grandchildren, mom, dad, or three brothers) would die. But with my dad, I didn't grieve like I thought I should. So, I took a real close look at why we hurt emotionally and physically when we lose a loved one.

We Were Never Made to Be Separated

Why do we grieve? I can now tell you why we grieve when we separate from
someone because of death. Everyone on Earth grieves when they lose someone they love, to death. We all do it differently, but we all do it. Sometimes, we don't even know we are doing it or accept that we are doing it.

As I stated earlier, through the story about Gloria Strout, we were never made to be separated, either spiritually or physically, as I stated in Chapter 4. The physical is governed through our five senses: touch, hearing, sight, smell, and taste. All of these senses were created to be ways to experience each other forever. When we were created male and female, our senses were made to intertwine with each other forever. We were created outside of time.

Genesis 1:26-28 (NKJV)
Then God said, "Let Us make man in Our image, according to Our likeness; let them have dominion over the fish of the sea, over the birds of the air, and over the cattle, over all the earth and over every creeping thing that creeps on the earth." So God created man in His own image; in the image of God He created him; male and female He created them. Then God blessed them, and God said to them, "Be fruitful and multiply; fill the earth and subdue it; have dominion over the fish of the sea, over the birds of the air, and over every living thing that moves on the earth."

As I just mentioned, we were made outside of time. Time was created at the same moment the earth and the universe were coming into existence. We can read this in Chapters 1 and 2 in the book of Genesis in the Bible. God, after a significant moment of creation, would make a statement, "There was evening, and there was morning, marking the first day." This first declaration is found in Genesis 1:5.

Genesis 1:5 (NET)
God called the light "day" and the darkness "night." There was evening, and there was morning, marking the first day.

God said this same statement in Genesis 1, verse 8 (second day), verse 13 (third day), verse 19 (fourth day), verse 23 (fifth day), and verse 31 (sixth day). Genesis 2:2-3 covers the seventh day. A day here is referred to as "time." Now, I am not in this to explain if the days are in twenty-four hour increments or in thousands of years. I just want you to see that time was here before humans were created. We didn't come into existence until the sixth day, really the last working day. On the sixth day, God made us outside of time. For we were brought into existence to live forever. Man was told what would throw him into time, which leads to physical and spiritual death. This is found in Genesis 2:16-17.

Genesis 2:16-17 (NET)
Then the LORD God commanded the man, "You may freely eat fruit from every tree of the orchard, but you must not eat from the tree of the knowledge of good and evil, for when you eat from it you will surely die."

We were placed in time because of what one man did – Adam. This caused us to die both physically and spiritually. But Jesus died so that we can live together forever. This is not only spiritual but also physical. We will each receive a new physical body in Heaven that won't fall apart or die.

Romans 5:18-21 (NKJV)
Therefore, as through one man's offense judgment came to all men, resulting in condemnation, even so through one Man's righteous act the free gift came to all men, resulting in justification of life. For as by one man's disobedience many were made sinners, so also by one Man's obedience many will be made righteous. Moreover the law entered that the offense might abound. But where sin abounded, grace abounded much more, so that as sin reigned in death, even so grace might reign through righteousness to eternal life through Jesus Christ our Lord.

Because of Jesus

So, because of Jesus, everyone on Earth has a chance to have that hope. What hope? That same hope that I have knowing that I will be with my dad again, forever. In Heaven, there is no separation from touching him, hearing his voice, seeing his face, smelling his fragrance, and tasting his presence – a complete spiritual connection outside of sin. I will get to once more experience my dad with my five senses. This is Good News!

We, who are Christians or born again, lose the interaction we have with those who have died, through our five senses, but we still encounter them spiritually. I knew when I came back to Earth that my body had died, but the real me (my spirit and soul) had not died. At first, I had a hard time grasping this because I had always believed that my physical being and my spiritual being really were not separate. I outwardly said that I understood that the two were separate, but inwardly I really didn't connect to what I read in the Bible about this subject. If you read your Bible, it states that you are both a spiritual and physical being. I understood it like most Christians do. Before I separated from my flesh, I acted like my physical body had a spirit on the inside, not like I was a spirit with a body on the outside. After I came back to Earth, after dying, I knew that we who are born again are spirits living inside bodies. Even though I was told that my flesh and spirit are fighting all the time for control over who I am or will be, I didn't fully grasp this concept at all. You can read about this battle in the Bible in the book of Romans in Chapters 7 and 8.

Here are a few verses from both of these chapters to help you get the gist of what we go through when we are born again.

Romans 7:5-6 (NET)
For when we were in the flesh, the sinful desires, aroused by the law, were active in the members of our body to bear fruit for death. But now we have been released from the law, because we have died to what controlled us, so that we may serve in the new life of the Spirit and not under the old written code.

Romans 8:7-8 (NET)
...because the outlook of the flesh is hostile to God, for it does not submit to the law of God, nor is it able to do so. Those who are in the flesh cannot please God

Now, I suggest that you read all of both chapters with the battle in mind.

Here's What Jesus Christ Did with the Battle in the Mind

Here is what Christ did for us who have accepted Him as Lord and Savior. He took the passions and desires of the flesh with him when He was crucified on the cross for our sins. He died with them so that we could be free if we choose to be.

Galatians 5:22-26 (NET)
But the fruit of the Spirit is love, joy, peace, patience, kindness, goodness, faithfulness, gentleness, and self-control. Against such things there is no law. Now those who belong to Christ have crucified the flesh with its passions and desires. If we live by the Spirit, let us also behave in accordance with the Spirit. Let us not become conceited, provoking one another, being jealous of one another.

2 Corinthians 5:17 (NET)
So then, if anyone is in Christ, he is a new creation; what is old has passed away – look, what is new has come!

So, what do we become after we are born again? We become free to live with the power to overcome our flesh, to not be subject to it in a way that is contrary to Christ.

This is true even with our spiritual connection through Jesus with others who are still alive with Him in Heaven.

Spiritual Connection Is Still There Through Jesus

On Earth, my dad had died. I love to say it this way: "He left the planet." Spiritually, I am still really connected to him through Jesus as John 15 states.

John 15:5 (NET)
"I am the vine; you are the branches. The one who remains in me – and I in him – bears much fruit, because apart from me you can accomplish nothing."

Because of Jesus, we who are born again are connected spiritually because Jesus is the vine and we are the branches, as I stated in chapter 4. Just like a grapevine that has branches that are connected through the trunk of the vine, so are we spiritually connected. Our flesh often gets in the way of a pure reading of this connection while we're here on Earth. So, we sometimes have a hard time reading the information we receive through this connection. In Heaven, I didn't have that problem because my earthly body didn't go with me. As I stated earlier, it was my spirit and soul that left my physical body here on Earth. Because of this, my flesh couldn't interfere with the pure essence of who I am. So, I tell people that I was connected to everything in

Heaven, and everything in Heaven was connected to me though Jesus Christ. I came back understanding that the spiritual connection we have is never broken. Even when a person dies on the planet, if they are born again or under the age of accountability spiritually, we are still connected through Jesus.

Sometimes on Earth We Experience That Connection

If a close family member is connected to us though Jesus, we are more aware of the signal we get through this connection. We even have it with children who are under the age of accountability. It's like when you just know that something is wrong with one of them, even when they are miles away from you. You may not know exactly what the problem is, but you know that something's not right. That is that spiritual connection. Even with someone who died and left the planet, we still have that spiritual connection through Jesus because spiritually they are not dead. Yes, they are with Jesus and our Heavenly Father in Heaven, but we are still connected with them through Jesus with the help of the Holy Spirit. That is why you may feel or sense that they are still alive.

Jesus tells us this in Matthew 22:29-33.

Matthew 22:29-33 (NKJV)
Jesus answered and said to them, "You are mistaken, not knowing the Scriptures nor the power of God. For in the resurrection they neither marry nor are given in marriage, but are like angels of God in heaven. But concerning the resurrection of the dead, have you not read what was spoken to you by God, saying, 'I am the God of Abraham, the God of Isaac, and the God of Jacob'? God is not the God of the dead, but of the living." And when the multitudes heard this, they were astonished at His teaching.

So, if we who are Christians have this connection, why do we still grieve over them? Because we still experience some loss. That is the way it was for me with my dad, not a lot but some. I just felt he left Earth. He was not dead, but from an earthly point of view, he died. So, that is when and how I came to understand the "spiritual connection" versus "the physical connection." Because I had died physically but not spiritually, the whole grief process started to make sense to me.

Spiritually Connected from Heaven to Earth

When I was in Heaven, I was still connected with my family on Earth. If it could happen from Heaven to Earth, could it not happen from Earth to Heaven? Yes it could. I never felt my dad was dead. I knew he died on Earth, but he was alive in Jesus. He was not just a memory to me, he was a living person. Even though he was in Heaven, with his Heavenly Father, he still was so alive to me. This is hard to understand for those who do not have a connection with Jesus. But for we who are born again – we who accept Jesus into our lives by confessing with our mouths and believing in our hearts and have the Holy Spirit residing on the inside of us – we have that connection whether we want it or not. It comes with being born again. Now this is Good News! Because of Jesus, spiritually I was still linked to my dad.

We Who Are Born Again, Why Do We Grieve?

So, why did I grieve some? Because I could no longer have physical touch with him. I couldn't see him anymore on Earth. I could no longer hear his voice. I couldn't smell him or sense his taste. We were created to be able to have interconnection with each other forever. What we now lose on Earth when someone we love dies is that connection through the five senses. It has been proven that we need all these five senses to be fully connected to someone we love. They also need them to connect to us.

PHYSICAL CONTACT Was Meant to Be Forever

Let's start with touch. Human physical contact in love can increase healthy lives mentally. Many people receive comfort when someone just puts their hand on their shoulder or hugs them. I know this is not true for everyone, but I just want to point out that touching is important to most human beings. Now, take that away and watch the grieving take place.

We were supposed to be able to have that physical contact forever. When we lose that option in our lives, we feel the loss. This is what I was feeling about my dad, and it is also what my family felt when I died for that 1 hour and 45 minutes. We need it now, and we need it forever. It is a connection that gives life to us if done in love. God even emphasizes the importance of physical touch in healing.

Mark 16:18c (NET)
"they will place their hands on the sick and they will be well."

God knew that man needed a physical companion to live with on Earth.

Genesis 2:18 (NET)
The LORD God said, "It is not good for the man to be alone. I will make a companion for him who corresponds to him."

Man and woman were made to come together to produce life – children. The primary way we were to help create life was through physical contact.

Genesis 1:28a (NET)
God blessed them and said to them, "Be fruitful and multiply!

Genesis 9:1 (NET)
Then God blessed Noah and his sons and said to them, "Be fruitful and multiply and fill the earth."

We all started out with physical contact when we were inside of our mothers. Why would we not need touch?

It has been proven by research that we have a hard time as humans when we go without physical contact in love. Years ago, I remember reading about babies who were born in Russia who were abandoned by their parents and placed in orphanages. Even in the orphanages, they were not held. They were fed, clothed, and cleaned, but they had no physical contact in love. The results were that many of the children became lifeless, and some died because of the lack of physical affection.

My little grandchildren love that contact from their parents, their grandmother, and of course their grandfather, me. Now understand something here. I love their contact with me too. Even the times when I am just bending down to tie my shoes and they jump on my back like I'm some kind of an outdoor toy. That physical connection is very important to me from my wife, family, and friends.

We Were Meant to HEAR Each Other Forever

Another reason we grieve is that we were meant to hear each other's voices forever. We have a great need to hear the voice of someone we love. It gives us a connection with them that helps us to feel a part of them.

I travel throughout the United States and the world. Sometimes, I'm gone away from Marilyn for a few days and other times for few weeks. Wherever I go away, I make time to talk to her by phone. I have noticed that sometimes when I talk to her, I really have nothing to say. It is like we don't have a thing to talk about, but I know I need to make that call. Why? Because I need to hear her voice. There are times when she has texted me goodnight, and I have tried to find a way to call her back. I didn't want to text her back, but I wanted to say goodnight with my voice; and I also wanted to hear her voice. It is a deep comfort to me to hear the sound of her voice on the other end of the line. I can even recognize her voice in a crowd of people talking. I have been separated from her when in a store and found her by just listening for the sound of her voice.

I have found this to be true with anyone who I have a close relationship with. My father (when he was alive on earth), mother, children, grandchildren, brothers, close friends, and anyone else who I have built a loving connection with – I love to hear their voices. If you think about it, I believe that you will find that you're most likely the same way.

As you have read, my dad went home to be with Jesus in April 2017. My mother misses him dearly. They were married for 63 years. Whenever I visit my mom, she reminds me of the many things she misses about my dad. One of the biggest things that she misses is hearing his voice. She looks so sad when talking about it. Not hearing that voice that she had heard for over 63 years brings her grief, and why not? At times, it brought her great comfort, and now there is an interruption in hearing his voice. Her eternal thinking was that she would always hear her husband's sound. She is born again and has the hope that she will see and hear my dad again, but for right now, it hurts to not be able to talk to him or hear him speak.

The Bible says our voices are important. In the book of Song of Solomon, we have some examples of how important the human voice is to us. According to the New English Translation Bible, the book of Song of Solomon is an allegorical poem that sets forth the mutual love of Christ and the Church, under the emblem of the bridegroom and the bride. So it is taking the first institution created by God, marriage, and using it as an example of how important having a relationship with Jesus is for both Him and us. When you read about the voice in the following verses, remember if our voices are valuable to God, then it must be important for us to hear each other's voices, too.

Song of Solomon 2:14 (NET)
The Lover to His Beloved: "O my dove, in the clefts of the rock, in the hiding places of the mountain crags, let me see your face, let me hear your voice; for your voice is sweet, and your face is lovely."

Song of Solomon 8:13 (NET)
The Lover to His Beloved: "O you who stay in the gardens, my companions are listening attentively for your voice; let me be the one to hear it!"

We Were Created to SEE Each Other Forever

When I was in Heaven, I did see other people who I had known on Earth. These were the redeemed, people who had accepted Jesus Christ as Lord and Savior. Even my whole family came to greet me in. How do I describe them? They were shiny because Jesus Christ was shining out of them. The had big smiles because they had no worries. And lastly, they had pure joy because of the way they looked overall. There, I didn't see them the same way that I had seen them here on Earth.

When I hold questions and answers services, one of the most frequently asked questions that I'm asked is this: "What do people look like in Heaven?" So many people who have lost loved ones want to see them in Heaven. I give them the answer of what my family looked like. As I said before, they were shiny, had big smiles, and had pure joy. Another frequently asked question (usually in private) is: "Did you see any of my relatives there?" I could tell when someone asked that question that there was a great need for that person not only to know that their relative was there in Heaven but also that they would see them again. Their next question was almost always: "What did they look like?"

At first, I couldn't understand why my having seen someone's family member in Heaven was so important to them, if they already knew they were there. Later, I came to understand why it was so important to so many people here on Earth. It is because we were made to look on each other's faces forever.

Again, in the book of Song of Solomon, we read how important it is to see each other's face.

Song of Solomon 2:14 (NET)
The Lover to His Beloved: "O my dove, in the clefts of the rock, in the hiding places of the mountain crags, let me see your face, let me hear your voice; for your voice is sweet, and your face is lovely."

Also, Paul, in all of his letters to the different churches, expressed in writing how he longed to see the believers in person. In 2 Timothy 1:1-4, he told Timothy how much he wanted to see him.

2 Timothy 1:1-4
Paul, an apostle of Jesus Christ by the will of God, according to the promise of life which is in Christ Jesus, To Timothy, a beloved son: Grace, mercy, and peace from God the Father and Christ Jesus our Lord. I thank God, whom I serve with a pure conscience, as my forefathers did, as without ceasing I remember you in my prayers night and day, greatly desiring to see you, being mindful of your tears, that I may be filled with joy,

Paul said he wanted to see Timothy so that his joy may be filled. In these verses, we read that seeing someone you love can bring you great joy.

I love seeing those I love, especially my family members, even if I disagree with them on some issues in life. I deeply love my family on Earth. When I came back from seeing my family in

Heaven, I understood how important family is to God! Through my experience, I grew in my love for every family member, even those who do not follow God like I do. I remember my Grandmother Mary saying, "Bring as many of us back with you as you can." I knew she wanted to see and be with as many of her family members as possible in Heaven.

We Were Created to SMELL Each Other Forever

A smell can be positive or negative. A good or bad smell leaves an imprint of a moment in our memory. Scent is one of the most powerful of the five senses, warning us of danger, triggering cherished memories, and even helping us to find our true love. For example, when I went to New Zealand, I came into contact with so many wonderful fragrances. Since that trip was such an outstanding experience for me, when back in the United States, if I smell any aroma even close to one that I smelled in New Zealand, it helps to bring back great memories of that trip. I can even remember sounds and surroundings of where I was in New Zealand. It seems that a fragrance can help you picture a place where you smelled it before. It works the same way with people.

It is estimated that worldwide beauty and personal care products generated sales valued at 465 billion US dollars in 2017. That tells us that to the human race the sense of smell is very important. Why would it not be if it is one of the biggest identifiers of truly understanding a thing, food, or person? It helps us to fully see or experience something as good or bad. Think about how many times a day smell triggers a memory from your past.

Intimate Time

Because we put so much time and money into smelling good, the scent of a person can be very intimate. This is why people buy expensive perfumes – to leave a good smell about themselves with others. We are aware of the importance of smelling good when it comes to personal relationships with people, both male and female. I can still remember when I was dating as a teenager, wanting to smell good, even my breath. I wanted to leave a scent with that person that left a good memory of me.

Even when fragrances are described in the Bible, it is in an intimate way. In 2 Corinthians verses 15-16, in a loving relationship with God, smell is used to describe a close encounter with Him.

2 Corinthians 2:15-16
For we are a sweet aroma of Christ to God among those who are being saved and among those who are perishing – to the latter an odor from death to death, but to the former a fragrance from life to life. And who is adequate for these things?

In these verses, it says that even to God we give off a good smell.

Our prayers are even described as incense, a smell, in Revelation 5:8.

Revelation 5:8 (NKJV)
Now when He had taken the scroll, the four living creatures and the twenty-four elders fell down before the Lamb, each having a harp, and golden bowls full of incense, which are the prayers of the saints.

My Wife

Marilyn shared with me what she went through when I died. One of the incidents she told me about had to do with her sense of smell. She told me about one time after she had left the hospital late at night and gotten home and was really tired. Now this took place after I had already died, and the doctors had me on life support. She would go to the hospital in the daytime and return back home at night to pray for me. Well, this particular night after she got home, she went into the house and went upstairs to our bedroom. When she entered the room, she opened my closet door and could smell my clothes, which had my scent on them. She started to get sad and heard in her head, "Get the funeral ready." She said that immediately she brought her thoughts into captivity to the obedience of Christ and told the devil that he was a liar. She continued to thank God for His promise, found in Psalm 103:3, for forgiving all my iniquities and healing all my diseases.

So, by the scent on my clothes, she had a negative reaction. I found out that it is hard for people who have lost a loved one to get rid of their clothes. This is not only because they are not ready to be parted from them but also because they can still smell the person's fragrance on their clothing.

We all produce good and bad smells, but the good scent was meant for us to smell forever.

We Were Created to TASTE Each Other Forever

The last sense I want to cover is taste. Really, this one goes along with smell. I even make the statement that I can't give you a great picture of Heaven because I can't tell you what it smelled like or what it tasted like. This is mainly because of how the smell and taste of death infiltrates itself into all life on Earth. This is why I often use Bible verses when telling the story of what it was like for me to die and go to Heaven.

To get a good picture of anything, you have to have the fullness of all your senses working for you. You may have seen dogs do this. They not only have to hear, see, and touch you, but they also have to smell and taste (lick) you. That's the way that they get the full picture of who you are.

We do this with people we love. With the smell they give off, there is a taste. This way, we can perceive the fullness of a person. I am not advocating for people to lick each other to fully know each other but to understand that we do taste each other. Most of the time, we do it with a kiss. Those we love a lot, we kiss. In that kiss, we taste. That taste was meant to be forever.

We are told to taste God like a good meal.

Psalm 34:7-8 (NET)
The LORD's angel camps around the LORD's loyal followers and delivers them. Taste and see that the LORD is good! How blessed is the one who takes shelter in him!

Even though taste is used as a metaphor in The New English Translation, it still appears to compare the Lord to a tasty meal.

Tasting something is important to us. Most people have 10,000 taste buds. It is said that as you get older, you end up with about 5,000. I may have been one of those who started out with less than 10,000. The reason that I say this is that I am around a whole lot of people, some who are family members, who love the taste of good food. When I am with them, they love to talk about the savoriness of their food. I call them "foodies" because of how they make a big deal over their food. My dad would make statements that kind of sum up what "foodies" are about. He would say, "Some people eat to live, and some people live to eat." I believe that I fall into the category of eating to live. "Foodies" will say that they live to eat, but I think they live to taste.

Again, we find out the word taste is used in Song of Solomon in the Bible as a way to have intimacy with someone we love.

Song of Solomon 2:3 (NET)
The Beloved about Her Lover: Like an apple tree among the trees of the forest, so is my beloved among the young men. I delight to sit in his shade, and his fruit is sweet to my taste.

We were meant to be able to have the sense of taste with us, for each other, forever.

Senses Are Supposed to Be with Us Forever

All of the senses were created to be with us forever in a superior way. They were given to human beings so that they would to be able to develop relationships and have fellowship with God and others. In the following verses, you will see that we had our five senses before we were subject to death.

Physical Touch
Physical Touch: "Be fruitful and multiply!" Back then, you had to have physical touch to be fruitful and multiply.

Genesis 1:28 (NET)
God blessed them and said to them, "Be fruitful and multiply! Fill the earth and subdue it! Rule over the fish of the sea and the birds of the air and every creature that moves on the ground."

Sight
Sight: God made us in an image to be able to be seen forever.

Genesis 1:27 (NET)
God created humankind in his own image, in the image of God he created them, male and female he created them.

Hearing
Hearing: God blessed them and spoke to them. They heard from God.

Genesis 1:28 (NET)
God blessed them and said to them, "Be fruitful and multiply! Fill the earth and subdue it! Rule over the fish of the sea and the birds of the air and every creature that moves on the ground."

Smell
Smell: The first smell a human smelled was the breath of life from God into his nostrils.

Genesis 2:7 (NET)
The LORD God formed the man from the soil of the ground and breathed into his nostrils the breath of life, and the man became a living being.

Taste
Taste: Where do we find taste before the sin of a man? When female and male ate from the tree of knowledge good and evil. As they ate, they tasted it.

Genesis 3:6 (NET)
When the woman saw that the tree produced fruit that was good for food, was attractive to the eye, and was desirable for making one wise, she took some of its fruit and ate it. She also gave some of it to her husband who was with her, and he ate it.

Why Do We Grieve?

Here we read that all five senses were imported into both the male and female when they were created. So, when we who are born again lose a loved one on Earth, we grieve because we have lost the connection of the five senses with that person. We still have the spiritual connection as I pointed out before, but we don't have the connection with the nature senses here on the planet. Because of that separation, we experience pain, which we call grieving.

But as I said earlier, we who are born again, we who call ourselves Children of God, have Hope. We have a promise that we will be with our loved ones again. Through Jesus Christ, we will not only know they are alive, but we will be able to touch, see, hear, smell, and taste them again. In Genesis1:26, God created people to be together forever. One man (Adam) messed it up, and one man (Jesus) fixed(s) it.

1 Thessalonians 4:13 (NET)
Now we do not want you to be uninformed, brothers and sisters, about those who are asleep, so that you will not grieve like the rest who have no hope.

Prayer for Salvation

I know that I have done things that were wrong, and I am sorry for all of them. I believe Jesus died on the cross for all my wrongdoings. I ask you, God, to please forgive me for all of them right now. I now receive you as my own Savior and Lord. With your help, Father God, I will try to please you every day of my life from this day forward. In Jesus' name, I thank you for saving me.

Chapter 6

Medical Records and Medical Transcripts

Before this incident took place, I was a very healthy 47-year-old male. I had regular physicals, and most of them were done because I was in the United States Air Force on active duty for 6 years and reserve duty for 14 years. I retired from the Air Force Reserves with a clean bill of health. The only health problem I had after that was kidney stones in June of 2002, four years prior to this incident.

I went through the same procedure back then for kidney stones as I did for this incident. The biggest difference was that I had to stay in the hospital overnight before this operation. In June of 2002, I checked into the hospital in the morning and left in the afternoon of the same day.

During the next four years after my first treatment for kidney stones, I didn't have any problems with kidney stones or any other illnesses. I do not remember taking any sick leave for personal illness during those years. I was a very healthy man up to this incident.

The following is taken from the Medical Records we received from both hospitals that I was admitted to. Now, getting these records was not easy because of the mistakes that had been made and the potential for a lawsuit. The doctor who made the mistakes made it hard for us to receive accurate reports. Finally, we were able to get other doctors who had worked on my case to give us information.

It was never our intention to sue either the doctor or the hospital. We just wanted the official medical records to support the medical testimonies we had received from the doctors, nurses, and other people who had worked in the hospitals.

Excerpts of information taken from my Medical Records and Medical Transcripts:

Preoperative Diagnosis: Left ureteral calculus and bilateral nephrolithiasis (kidney stones) and pyelonephritis (urinary tract infection)

Postoperative Diagnosis: Left ureteral calculus and bilateral nephrolithiasis and pyelonephritis

Operation: Cystoscopy with retrograde pyelogram, push back of ureteral calculus and bilateral extracorporeal shock wave lithotripsy

Indications: This delightful 49-year-old gentleman (really 47-year-old) presented to the hospital with pyelonephritis and obstruction ureteral calculus. After 24 hours of antibiotic coverage with supplemental antibiotic administration in operation room, he presents at this time for definitive surgical intervention.

Findings: Obstructing calculus in the left ureter is pushed back in the renal pelvis, and a 24-cm 7-french double-J stent is left in place in the ureter and that calculus further targets and both kidneys were fragmented with difficulty. After 2,400 shocks, the procedure was terminated, and the patient was awakened and returned to the recovery room in satisfactory condition. There were no complications. He tolerated the procedure well. This was from a May 6, 2006, report by the surgeon who performed the original operation.

Excerpts taken from the rest of the Medical Records and Medical Transcripts:

Larger amount of fluid resuscitation for hypertension
Poorly responsive
Moves legs to pain
Very cool digits with cyanotic toes
Acute renal failure
Secondary to acute tubular necrosis oliguric
Profound septic shock
Prolonged cardiac arrest
CPR one 1 and 45 minutes
Septic shock with urasepisis
Respiratory failure
Pulmonary infiltrates
Edema versus adult respiratory distress syndrome
Post prolonged CPR

Post cardiac arrest
Prolonged resuscitation
Fulminant sepsis
Too numerous to count – stones in right kidney
Chest x-rays show the development of diffuse pulmonary edema
Urine culture sent yesterday is growing greater than 100,000
colonies of E. coli.
Doctor reports spent a total of 1 hour and 45 min. total critical
care time with the patient not including procedure
Severe sepsis
Diagnosis of SIRS/Sepsis with hypotension, tachycardia,
tachypnea, hypoxemia.
High risk of disseminated intravascular coagulation.
Cardiac arrest
Urasepsis with E. Coli.
Secondary renal shut down.
Asystable
Extubated
Herodynamically Stable
Shock liver
Shock syndrome
Hemodynamic stress
On mechanical ventilation
Paralytic ileus
Multi-organ failure
Critically ill
Prognosis is poor
Quinton Catheter and dialysis treatment (risk & benefits)
Risk for bleeding complication with ongoing DIC
Clotting dialysis system given ongoing DIC
Obstruction urinary stones
Severely acidotic with a lactic acid as high as 16
Poorly responsive
Requiring High Fi0 Moderate to servers patchy air space
Opacities in the lungs bilaterally slightly increased. This is
worrisome for progression of pneumonia.
Very unfortunate critically ill patient

After the recovery, I wanted the first doctor to remove
the stent that he had placed in my body, but he was resistant to
the idea. My wife had to call the doctor and state that she was
going to take legal action if we did not receive an appointment to

have this procedure done. We were scheduled for an appointment the following day, and the doctor removed the stent.

I asked him at that time what had happened to cause my heart to stop. He told me that I had a bad infection that he thought was taken care of with some really strong medicine. But, for some reason, the infection was not affected by the medicine that had been given to me. He said that they had not checked prior to the operation whether the medicine had worked or not, and they had assumed that it did. It wasn't until five days later that they found out from lab reports that the medicine didn't have any effect on the kidney infection.

At the time of the incident, the doctor didn't know what was going wrong or why my vital organs were shutting down. He told me that if they hadn't done everything right, I would have been behind the eight ball (dead). If they had done a process ten minutes earlier or ten minutes later, I would have died.

I did ask him if I had died. He said my heart had stopped and that every time it looked like it was going to start, it didn't. He said they worked on me for about 1 hour and 30 minutes (Official record states 1 hour and 45 minutes). I asked him if he saw this as a miracle, and he said that it was and that I should go tell the story.

As you can see, there were a lot of things that just went wrong with the procedures and with my body, and I DIED!

Prayer for Salvation

I know that I have done things that were wrong, and I am sorry for all of them. I believe Jesus died on the cross for all my wrongdoings. I ask you, God, to please forgive me for all of them right now. I now receive you as my own Savior and Lord. With your help, Father God, I will try to please you every day of my life from this day forward. In Jesus' name, I thank you for saving me.

Don't Tell Me Good-Bye
By Christy A. Ostrander
3/13/17

As the shadows gently close in on me
And I run toward the distant light
There no more will sorrow be
And the Lord shall be my delight

I know that I shall see
His most glorious face
Smiling radiantly upon me
And death will no more have its place
For Christ has won the victory

So please don't tell me good-bye
For this is not my end
I don't want to see you cry
But I must hurry on my way
For Jesus is waiting for me my friend

And even though I'm gone from you
I know that He will stay so true
He will help you fight your battles and will never leave your side
Stay with Him and He will see you through
Till death will close your eyes
But fear not! For there's just one more surprise

So please, don't tell me good-bye
For this is not the end
No matter how hard death may try
So please hurry on your way
For Jesus is waiting for you my friend

My Dad's Morning Prayer
By St. Richard of Chichester

Lord Jesus, bless my memory
this day, that it may ever
recollect You.

Bless my understanding,
that it may ever think of You.
Bless my will that it may never seek, nor desire that which
may be displeasing to you.
Bless my body with all its actions.
Bless my heart with its affections.
Bless me now and at the hour
of my death.

Bless my dear ones.
Bless everyone I love and everyone
to whom I owe any gratitude,
and bring me and them to rest
In Your Sacred Heart forever.

Prayer for Salvation

I know that I have done things that were wrong, and I am
sorry for all of them. I believe Jesus died on the cross for all my
wrongdoings. I ask you, God, to please forgive me for all of them
right now. I now receive you as my own Savior and Lord. With
your help, Father God, I will try to please you every day of my life
from this day forward. In Jesus' name, I thank you for saving me.

Made in United States
North Haven, CT
15 September 2024

57492493R00050